State Parks
of California
from 1864 to the present

S0-BUB-177

Berry Creek Falls, Big Basin Redwoods State Park.

STATE PARKS OF CALIFORNIA

from 1864 to the present

Text by Joseph H. Engbeck, Jr.

Color Photography by Philip Hyde

"As the centuries pass, the mystery of the Universe deepens. The thoughts of civilised man accumulate like snowflakes on the summit of Everest, or the leaves of many years in winter woods, burying one past system after another, one fashion after another in religion, science, poetry and art. Knowing that so much lies buried beneath, which but now was so hot and certain, it becomes ever more difficult to trust so implicitly as of old whatever still for the moment lies on the surface of human thought, the still surviving dogma, or the latest fashion in opinion. At least it becomes difficult to trust either to dogma or to thought alone. Man looks round for some other encouragement, some other source of spiritual emotion that will not be either a dogma or a fashion, something

"That will be forever,
That was from of old."

And then he sees the sunset, or the mountains, the flowing river, the grass and trees and birds on its banks. In the reality of these he cannot fail to believe, and in these he finds, at moments, the comfort that his heart seeks."

Professor G. M. Trevelyan
"The Call and Claims of Natural Beauty," 1931

International Standard Book Number
0-912856-39-4

Library of Congress
Catalog Number
78-51220

Printed in the United States of America

Copyright ©1980
by Graphic Arts Center Publishing Co.

2000 N.W. Wilson Street
Portland, Oregon 97209
503/224-7777

Publisher • Charles H. Belding

Color Separations and Printing by:
Graphic Arts Center, Portland

Typography by:
Paul O. Giesey/Adcrafters, Portland

Binding by:
Lincoln and Allen

Design by:
John Beyer, San Francisco

Contents

Burney Falls, McArthur—Burney Falls Memorial State Park

Castle Crags State Park.

Picture Credits:

All of the full color photographs used in this book are by Philip Hyde, Taylorsville, California.

The painting by Albert Bierstadt, page 16, has been reproduced here through the courtesy of the Timken Art Gallery, the Putnam Foundation, San Diego, California.

All black and white photographs other than those listed below are from the files of the California Department of Parks and Recreation.

Photographs on the following pages have been reproduced through the courtesy of the Bancroft Library, University of California, Berkeley: 18, 19, 21, 22, 23, 24, 25, 26, 31, 32 top, 34, 35, 41, 43, 48 bottom, 49 top, 49 bottom, 83 middle, 95 bottom.

Pages 28, 29, 30 top, 30 bottom, and 33, courtesy of the Sempervirens Fund.

Page 32 bottom, courtesy of the San Jose Historical Museum.

Pages 45, 47, and 50 bottom, courtesy of the Save-the-Redwoods League.

Pages 38 bottom, 46, 50 top, 51, 52, 55, 62, 72 top, 77, and 90 top, from the personal collection of Newton B. Drury.

Pages 59, and 71 top, from the personal collection of Everett E. Powell.

Pages 60, 66 bottom, 71 bottom, and 78, from the personal collection of Earl Hanson.

Cartoons on pages 53, 54, and 57, courtesy of the Newspaper Room, the Doe Library, University of California, Berkeley.

Page 61 top, courtesy of Mrs. Edmund N. Brown.

Page 63, courtesy of the San Diego Historical Society, Title Insurance and Trust Collection.

Page 99, courtesy of the California Room, California State Library.

Page 102 top left, courtesy of Ray King.

Page 110 top, courtesy of the Department of the Interior, Bureau of Reclamation.

Page 110 bottom, courtesy of the California Department of Water Resources.

Preface

This book is an outgrowth of the California State Park System's 50th Anniversary Celebration of 1977-78. Preparations for that event made it apparent that very little reliable information was available about the creation of the park system during the 1920s. Only a few well-informed eyewitnesses remained; documentary evidence was alarmingly scant and widely scattered, very little of it in official archives. It seemed important that an effort be made to gather what material still existed, and that a report be compiled—an interesting and readable report, one that would be attractive and interesting to the public as well as to park professionals. A small illustrated book or booklet was in order.

As work got underway on the little "state park history book" it soon became clear that to be really useful the history should reach still further back in time to the state's first individually created and individually administered parks and historic monuments. And if this telling of the state park story were to really start at the beginning—as all good stories should—then it should also come marching all the way forward to the present so that readers might gain at least a general idea of how and why the California State Park System has come to be what it is today.

And so this book was written neither as a chronology nor as a travel guide; neither as a list of events nor as a catalogue of places and facilities. It does not pretend to be a thorough documentary report complete with footnotes and appendices; nor is it simply a light-hearted departmental history—an in-house document full of anecdotes and intimate personal sketches. (Though there is a wealth of such material available, some of which clearly deserves literary treatment.) Instead, this book is intended to be an illustrated and readable interpretive history of the California

State Park System and the movement that created it. Emphasis has been given to the ideas behind the movement and to the groups and individuals who took those ideas and turned them into the practical (and still evolving) reality that we know today as the California State Park System.

In so far as this book may prove to be of value, credit must be given to many people. First of all, it was Herb Rhodes, Director of the Department of Parks and Recreation in 1977, who first officially recognized the need—the public value—of such a book. He made the decision to launch this project. Special credit must also be given to Russ Cahill and Alice Huffman (formerly Alice Wright-Cottingim), who agreed with Herb Rhodes about the need for this kind of publication and later had the necessary patience, courage, and determination to see the project through despite all difficulties.

Credit should also be given to Earl Hanson who throughout his 40-year career in state parks personally preserved many unique and irreplaceable, official but "obsolete" documents that otherwise would have been destroyed by well-meaning but perhaps misguided governmental "housecleaners." A number of librarians were especially helpful including those associated with the California Room of the State Library in Sacramento and the extraordinary Bancroft Library at the University of California in Berkeley.

John DeWitt and the entire staff of the Save-the-Redwoods League were not only gracious and generous with their help—they were absolutely indispensable. The archives of the league (many of them now in the care of the Bancroft Library) turned out to hold more answers to more questions about the state park story than any other single source. Newton B. Drury himself, so long associated with the league, was also indispensable. He gave many hours of his valuable time to interviews and manuscript review, and not only provided eye-witness accounts of many crucial events, but was also willing to focus the light of his accumulated wisdom and perspective on those events. Though he was

invariably modest about his own role in the park movement, he was eager to see others properly credited, not so much in order to pay homage to them or to history, but rather in the hope that the park story, accurately presented, would inspire present and future supporters of the park movement to still greater accomplishment on behalf of the public. He continued to be helpful in his uniquely charming, calm, and lucid way right up to within a day or two of his death in December 1978.

Horace Albright, Lawrence Merriam, Joseph C. Houghteling, William Penn Mott, Jr., Richard M. and Doris Leonard, Claude A. "Tony" Look, Aubrey Neasham, Ray King, Edward F. Dolder, Earl Hanson, Everett E. Powell, Alice M. Garibaldi, Charles McLaughlin (editor of the Olmsted Papers), Jack Knight and many other current members of the California Department of Parks and Recreation, and still others far too numerous to mention here, all provided valuable information and insights into the historical record. The author is also grateful to all those who rendered quietly heroic service as typists, proof readers, editors, and reviewers.

On a personal note I would like to add that I have considered it a great honor to work on this project, and a great pleasure to meet and confer with so many of the people who have been most vitally involved in the California state park story. One of my greatest difficulties has been to decide what could be left out of this narrative in the name of brevity without seriously distorting the overall picture. In the final analysis, of course, it has been necessary to leave out almost everything. Only the bare bones—the highlights—remain. And some will no doubt wonder why one or another part of the story—perhaps their own part—is not told more fully. I can only hope that the story as presented here is well balanced. The intensity of commitment that parks inspire is ample assurance that many interesting and dramatic stories remain to be told.

Torrey Pines State Reserve.

Torrey Pines State Reserve.

Salt Point State Park.

Torrey Pines State Reserve.

Introduction

The California State Park System is today almost certainly the most diverse and wonderful system of its kind in the nation. It includes cool, dark redwood forests along the edge of the continent. It also includes broad stretches of stark and lonely, sunstruck desert land in the southeastern part of the state. There are magnificent alpine areas high in the Sierra Nevada, and there are many miles of ocean shoreline both along the beautiful but rugged north coast and along the gentle, warm, and sandy beaches of the south.

The system includes many landmarks—both official and unofficial—that give shape and meaning to life in California. The deeply weathered granite spires of Castle Crags are a milestone for every traveler along the main highway that follows the upper Sacramento River in northern California. The amazing spectacle of Burney Falls is a scenic highlight of the lava country in northeastern California. The breathtaking beauty of Emerald Bay at Lake Tahoe ranks among the scenic wonders of the world. Morro Rock on the central coast continues to be, as it has been for centuries, an important landmark for navigators both on land and sea. The horizon of the San Francisco Bay Region is defined and highlighted by two mountains, Mount Diablo and Mount Tamalpais, whose upper slopes and summits are protected and kept open to the public by state park status. In southern California, state park status protects the dramatic, often snowclad summit and upper reaches of Mount San Jacinto, which towers over Palm Springs and the Coachella Valley on the east, and over Los Angeles and the coastal plains and valleys to the west.

Officially designated historic landmarks—more than 800 of them—can be found in every corner of the state. They commemorate historic places and events that range from aboriginal village sites to 18th century Spanish missions, to nineteenth and twentieth century Mexican and American sites of many kinds. Historic buildings such as the chapel or the commandant's house at Fort Ross, the old Custom House in Monterey, the Franciscan missions at Sonoma and La Purisima, the old State Capitol at Benicia or the old

Founders Grove, Humboldt Redwood State Park.

Governor's Mansion in Sacramento, all help to keep history alive in the minds of California citizens. The homes of several well-loved and world famous individuals including Jack London and Will Rogers are being preserved and kept open for public viewing. And now, under the leadership of the State Office of Historic Preservation, complete historic districts are being recognized for their cultural and educational value and protected from heedless or unnecessary destruction.

The California State Park System also maintains a system of trails, and offers a wide range of other outdoor recreational opportunities in a wide range of environments including the man-made reservoir areas of the California Water Project. Recreational activity in these many areas includes hiking, nature study, fishing, swimming, boating, waterskiing, horseback riding, and even (in specially designated areas) the use off-road recreational vehicles.

Altogether, the California State Park System today includes some 250 individual park units with a total area of approximately one million acres. It represents the vision, idealism, and practical accomplishment of several generations of people both within and outside state government. Thousands of park rangers and other state employees have dedicated their entire careers to the park system. And countless private individuals and groups have given generously of their time and money and effort and thought. But, of course, the system is not perfect. Nor is it in any sense finished or complete. On the contrary, it is alive, dynamic,

Bodie State Historic Park.

La Purisima Mission State Historic Park.

11

The chapel, Fort Ross State Historic Park.

evolving—changing to meet the changing needs of contemporary society and of generations yet to come.

Perhaps the greatest challenge now facing the system, and the park movement in general, is the need to more adequately meet the recreational needs of those thousands of people in our urban centers who are not highly mobile. Such people find it difficult or impossible to enjoy the scenic, scientific, natural, historic, and recreational heritage that belongs equally to all Californians. The attempt to solve this prob-

lem has brought about a basic revision of park system priorities; the whole matter of urban parks is now a major preoccupation of state park planners and administrators.

This and other challenges facing the State Park System today are probably as difficult as any that have occurred in the past. Yet, looking back over the history of the state park movement, one cannot help but be optimistic about the future, for many of the accomplishments we take for granted today in the State Park System were the seeming impos-

sibilities of past moments. When one looks closely at how those impossibilities were overcome—when one looks at the people and the procedures, the hopes and dreams and ideals, that have made the park system what it is today —there remains little room for doubt that issues facing the park movement now and in the foreseeable future will tend to be resolved favorably.

Public parks and park-related matters are direct expressions of several basic American ideas about freedom, independence, social equity, and the

Left: *The chapel and palisade, Fort Ross State Historic Park.* Right: *Rock detail, Weston Beach, Point Lobos State Reserve.* Below: *Big Sur Coast, Julia Pfeiffer Burns State Park.*

Torrey Pines State Reserve.

Saddleback Butte State Park.

Providence Mountains State Recreation Area.

Red Rock Canyon State Recreation Area.

right to the pursuit of happiness. Parks and park-related matters attract the attention and concern of generous, public-spirited people who delight in seeing their ideals expressed in down-to-earth and practical ways. In California and in the nation at large this has been true throughout the last century and more. Simply on the basis of the record therefore, it seems likely that successive generations of practical idealists will continue to come forward, to involve themselves in state park matters, and find ways whereby the park movement can rise to meet the challenges that lie ahead.

How did the State Park System get to be the way it is? Who are the "practical idealists" who created and shaped it? And where does the story first begin?

Surprisingly enough, the California state park story begins not in a place we know today as a state park, but with Yosemite Valley and the Mariposa Grove of Big Trees, the first state park in the nation, and the first large scenic and natural area to be set aside by a central government on behalf of the people—the people, that is, not just of California, but of the nation and the world.

1 Yosemite, the First State Park

"...without means are taken by government to withhold them from the grasp of individuals, all places favorable to the recreation of the mind and body will be closed against the great body of the people."

Frederick Law Olmsted

"Camping in the Yosemite."
by Albert Bierstadt, 1864.
Oil on canvas, 34" x 27".

In the spring of 1864, with the nation divided and caught seemingly without end in the tragic violence of civil war, a unique piece of legislation quietly wound its way through the halls of Congress and onto the desk of President Abraham Lincoln. This legislation, authored by Senator John Conness of California, called for a grant to the State of California of some 20,000 acres of federal land in and completely surrounding the "cleft" or "gorge" known as the Yosemite Valley and the nearby Mariposa Big Tree Grove. Federal land grants to states and even to private corporations for economic and developmental purposes were not unusual, but this grant called for the preservation of natural conditions and protection of natural scenery. And it was made "upon the express conditions that the premises shall be held for public use, resort, and recreation, and shall be inalienable for all time."

Despite this unique statement of purpose, congressional discussion of the legislation was sedate and brief. And a few days after Congress approved the bill, President Abraham Lincoln signed it without public comment. The date was June 30, 1864.

Thus, quietly and without controversy, in the shadow of a dark moment in our national history, the nation's first state park was created. In retrospect this was clearly a momentous event in the history of the American park movement, and in later years many people have wondered how it was so easily and quickly accomplished, especially in light of the fact that subsequent park proposals were hotly contested even when they were of less magnitude and came after the precedent-setting Yosemite legislation. The answer will never be known with mathematical precision, but the question is worth examining, for it reveals a great deal not only about the creation of the park at Yosemite, but also about the role of parks in a democratic society.

First of all, it must be remembered that the Yosemite park idea was unopposed. At least in Washington, D.C. in 1864, no voice was given to local or special interests that might be injured by the proposed park. It should also be remembered that by 1864 the extraordinary scenery of Yosemite Valley and the Mariposa Grove of Big Trees was already well known to people in the eastern states, and in England and Europe, through sketches, paintings, photographs, and the extravagant reports of early visitors. Preserving and protecting the beauty of Yosemite was a way of proclaiming to everyone in all the states, north and south, and to the world at large, that the United States of America was fully aware of its newly won continental status, and proud not only of its rapid growth in population and wealth, but also of its matchless scenic resources. Even a scenic wonder in the remote mountains of the Far West was part of the nation. This was an especially important statement to make at a time when the very idea of the federal union was being challenged.

The federal grant also demonstrated, more eloquently than mere words could ever hope to do, that as a "democracy within a republic," the United States was committed to preserving its finest western scenery not for the short-term private profit of a few, but for the continuing, long-term benefit of the whole population.

All this was implicit in the Yosemite legislation at the time of its passage. And under other circumstances these ideas might well have been the subject of some stirring public rhetoric. But other, more urgent problems preoccupied the nation's leaders, especially during July and August of 1864, perhaps the darkest months of all in the prolonged agony of the Civil War. Nevertheless, the main ideas implicit in the Yosemite grant had been articulated or were otherwise clearly associated with the people who stood behind it. A quick look at the people most closely associated with the grant provides probably the best possible perspective on the goals and ideals that led to the creation of America's first large, natural park.

The People Behind the Grant

Frederick Law Olmsted was a writer and editor of national and international reputation. His careful, first-hand observations of the moral, ethical, practical, and economic disadvantages of slave-based agriculture in the ante-bellum South were widely known. He was also rather famous as the first superintendent and a principal designer of Central Park in New York City, the nation's first large-scale, central-city, people's park. Though he was an outspoken patriot, military service was out of the question, for an injury suffered in 1860 had left him with a badly crippled leg. In June 1861, after a diligent search for a significant way to serve the Union cause, Olmsted gave up his Central Park position to become chief executive and principal organizer of the Sanitary Commission, the forerunner of today's Red Cross. He served that organization with distinction—some called it heroism—until 1863 when an internal administrative disagreement caused him to leave the commission and accept a lucrative job offer in California. Thus it came about, luckily for everyone concerned, that Olmsted—perhaps the leading park man in America at the time—was managing the fabulous Mariposa Estate near Yosemite when the Yosemite park idea began to be discussed.

Thomas Starr King was a Unitarian minister from New England serving in California during the Civil War. He was well known in the East as a lecturer, and as a writer of delightful natural history articles, as well as a book about the White Mountains of New Hampshire. Soon after his arrival in California, King visited the Sierra Nevada and Yosemite Valley and wrote a series of very popular articles about them for an eastern newspaper. In California, under the pressure of the historical moment, King quickly came to be known as an outspoken patriot—California's most eloquent and persuasive spokesman for the Union cause—and as a major fund raiser for the Sanitary Commission. He opposed slavery on moral and spiritual grounds. And he argued, as many did, that the nation could not survive half slave and half free. Agreeing with Olmsted and other serious students of the man-nature relationship in America, he argued that it was not even possible to divide the nation, for it was held together by the immutable realities of its own geography, by its great rivers and valleys, fertile plains and scenic mountain ranges. On more than one occasion, Lincoln himself echoed this theme in speeches to Congress and the nation.

Unfortunately, King's unique role in California, Yosemite, and national affairs was cut short by sudden illness and death on March 4, 1864. His impact on the founders of the Yosemite Park, however, cannot be doubted. His is one of the very few personal names ever given to a major land feature in the Yosemite grant.

Jessie Benton Fremont was the extraordinarily capable and widely admired daughter of the longtime congressional leader and promoter of western expansion, Senator Thomas Hart Benton of Missouri. She was, moreover, the wife of the famous western explorer, "The Pathfinder," John C. Fremont, who in early 1864 made a determined bid to replace Lincoln as president. In earlier years the Fremonts had owned the seventy-square-mile Mariposa Estate outright. By 1864 they still had an interest in it—and the hope that with good luck and Olmsted's administrative genius the estate could still

Frederick Law Olmsted circa 1890.

The Colfax Party in Yosemite Valley, August 1865. Olmsted: second row, center. Colfax: second row, third from left. William Ashburner: front row, center.

be saved from the financial clouds that had gathered around it.

Josiah Dwight Whitney, an eminent chemist and geologist, and the man for whom Mount Whitney was later named, was in 1864 serving as director of the California State Geological Survey, and was thereby an important cog in the machinery of westward expansion and settlement. His influence went even beyond that, however, for he was a member of an extremely prominent east coast family which had among other accomplishments built a great commercial empire, and given Yale University three of its presidents.

Other backers of the Yosemite legislation included members of road-building, railroad, and steamship companies all of which were strongly interested in tourism, settlement, and development of the Far West. Thus it can be seen that the Yosemite legislation supporters and enthusiasts were not anti-development preservationists. On the contrary, they represented a wide range of important political and developmental interests.

On September 28, 1864, responding to the federal legislation, California Governor Frederick F. Low issued a proclamation announcing the federal grant, and commanding "all persons to desist from trespassing or settling upon said territory, and from cutting timber or doing any unlawful acts within the limits of the said grant." In the same proclamation, still following the terms of the federal legislation, he appointed an eight-member board of commissioners who would be unpaid, but who would assist him in managing the area. Heading the list was Frederick Law Olmsted, who was appointed by the governor not only to serve on the commission, but also to handle "all propositions for the improvement" of the grant,

and any leases that might be desired by prospective concessionaires. The other members of what was, in effect, California's first state park commission were: J. D. Whitney, William Ashburner, I. W. Raymond, E. S. Holden, Alexander Deering, George W. Coulter, and Galen Clark.

Although nearly two years would pass before the state legislature would confirm California's formal acceptance of the grant, Olmsted set to work immediately. The first step called for by the federal legislation was a survey and map of Yosemite Valley that would clearly establish the precise boundaries of the new reserve. Since state funds were not available, Olmsted advanced $500 of his own personal funds for the purpose. As a result, boundary surveying and map work were completed in the autumn of 1864 and promptly filed with the General Land Office.

On behalf of the commission, Olmsted also set out to determine and describe an appropriate and wise management policy for the federal grant which was, after all, completely without precedent—unique in all the world. The word "park" was not even associated as yet with Yosemite or any other wilderness area. In order to do the job properly, Olmsted wanted to be personally familiar with the area, and so in July and August, even before the governor's proclamation was made public, he took his family and a number of friends and spent several weeks camping out and exploring the Mariposa Grove of Big Trees, Yosemite Valley, and the surrounding Yosemite high country. A thoughtful and loving observer of natural landscapes, Olmsted subsequently described the scenery of the high Sierra as "the grandest I ever saw." Yosemite Valley itself, he said

without qualification, was "the greatest glory of nature."

The Origin of National and State Park Policy

The administrative and policy problem Olmsted had to grapple with was how best to preserve the unique natural values of Yosemite Valley while at the same time opening the area to public use. In all the nation there was probably no one better qualified to deal with this problem. Not only was he sensitive to aesthetic matters—to scenery and its visual impact on human beings—he was also interested in botanical, geological, and other natural values. He was, moreover, a longtime, eager student of parks and park administration both in America and Europe. Another important and often overlooked factor, however, is that Olmsted was a keen observer of American civilization, a man who, through his writing and editing for various leading journals of the day, had tested his ideas and opinions in the intellectual marketplace.

During his Yosemite trip and throughout the following year, Olmsted took every opportunity to confer with engineers, road builders, architects, artists, painters, photographers, botanists, geologists, and other experts whose advice was relevant to the Yosemite question. Though there was still no immediate prospect of an appropriation by the State of California, he again advanced his own personal funds in order to have a detailed map of the valley prepared for planning and management purposes. Finally, in August 1865, he presented his plan and policy statement to the Yosemite Commission at its first official meeting in the valley itself.

As fortune would have it, the meeting was attended by a distinguished group of visitors including Schuyler Colfax, Speaker of the House of Representatives, Lieutenant Governor William Bross of Illinois, Charles Allen, Attorney General of Massachusetts, Samuel Bowles, editor of the Springfield (Mass.) Republican, and other leading journalists of the time.

Although Olmsted's report was never officially presented to the legislature by the commission, it nevertheless deserves close scrutiny, for it is one of the most interesting and compelling statements ever written about the park idea. The report remained unpublished for nearly 90 years, but a single copy (perhaps two) of Olmsted's manuscript was preserved and used for later reference. Furthermore, several of the distinguished visitors who listened to Olmsted as he read his report that day in Yosemite carried his ideas home to eastern audiences that included many influential people. Altogether, the impact of the report should not be underestimated.

In his report, Olmsted described the main features of the site itself and then went on to present the basic philosophical, political, and economic justifications for state and national parks in a democratic society. "First and least important," he said, "is the direct and obvious pecuniary advantage which comes to a commonwealth from the fact that it possesses objects . . . that are attractive to travelers and the enjoyment of which is open to all." He reminded his audience that the tourism industry of Switzerland was the envy of nations all around the world. Heavy capital investment in art objects and museums was unnecessary if a country was blessed with a scenic attraction such as Yosemite Valley, which was already beginning to attract visitors from Europe and other parts of the world despite its relative inaccessibility and lack of tourist accommodations.

Second, and more important according to Olmsted, public ownership and development of Yosemite and other scenic areas by the government was "a political duty of grave importance to which seldom if ever before has proper respect been paid by any government in the world, but the grounds of which rest on the same eternal base of equity and benevolence with all other duties of republican government.

"It is the main duty of government, if it is not the sole duty of government, to provide means of protection for all its citizens in the pursuit of happiness against the obstacles, otherwise insurmountable, which the selfishness of individuals or combinations of individuals is liable to interpose to that pursuit.

"It is a scientific fact that the occasional contemplation of natural scenes of an impressive character, particularly if this contemplation occurs in connection with relief from ordinary cares, change of air and change of habits, is favorable to the health and vigor of men and especially to the health and vigor of their intellect beyond any other conditions which can be offered them, that it not only gives pleasure for the time being but increases the subsequent capacity for happiness and the means of securing happiness."

This fact of life, Olmsted said, had been known and acted upon by men of wealth and privilege throughout recorded history. "The great men of the Babylonians, the Persians and the Hebrews, had their rural retreats, as large and as luxurious as those of the aristocracy of Europe at present." But if the "enjoyment of the choicest natural scenes in the country and the means of recreation connected with them" is only available to the owners of private estates, then it is "a monopoly, in a very peculiar manner, of a very few, very rich people. The great mass of society, including those to whom it would be the greatest benefit, is excluded from it. In the nature of the case private parks can never be used by the mass of the people in any country nor by any considerable number even of the rich, except by the favor of a few, and in dependence on them.

"Thus without means are taken by government to withhold them from the grasp of individuals, all places favorable in scenery to the recreation of the mind and body will be closed against the great body of the people. For the same reason that the water of rivers should be guarded against private appropriation and . . . otherwise protected against obstruction, portions of natural scenery may therefore properly be guarded and cared for by government."

Olmsted went on to point out that Congress had set aside the Yosemite grant not only for these broad political and philosophical considerations, but also because of its unique natural scenery. The first responsibility of the Yosemite Commission, therefore, was to protect the scenic and natural values of the area. "This duty of preservation is the first which falls upon the state under the Act of Congress, because the millions who are hereafter to benefit by the Act have the largest interest in it, and the largest interest should be first and most strenuously guarded. . . . In permitting the sacrifice of anything that would be of the slightest value to future visitors to the convenience, bad taste, playfulness, carelessness, or wanton destructiveness of present visitors, we probably yield in each case the interest of uncounted millions to the selfishness of a few individuals." In keeping with this point of view, Olmsted concluded that development of the valley for public use should interfere as little as possible with the natural scene. He therefore recommended construction of narrow, one-way roads that would enable visitors to travel all around the valley. He argued that such relatively narrow roads would be more pleasant to use, cheaper to build, easier to maintain, and at the same time do less damage to the natural scene than conventional two-way roads. He also described the accommodations and public services that should be provided in the valley, and outlined the regulations that would be necessary to preserve the scenery for present and future generations.

According to Olmsted, the next most important responsibility of the commission after protecting scenic and natural values was to make the area accessible to the public. If Congress had not specifically reserved the valley for public use, Olmsted pointed out, "it would have been practicable for one man to have bought the whole, to have appropriated it wholly to his individual pleasure or to have refused admittance to any who were unable to pay a certain price as admission fee, or as a charge for the entertainment which he would have had a monopoly of supplying. The result would have been a rich man's park. . . ." But so long as access remained as time-consuming and difficult as it then was, the area would

"The Three Brothers," Yosemite Valley. Photo by Carleton E. Watkins.

"remain, practically the property of only the rich."

Olmsted believed that supplies should be brought in both for visitors and for the horses, mules, and other livestock belonging to visitors. If supplies were not provided, Olmsted feared it would be difficult or impossible to prevent visitors from cutting down trees for firewood and turning their livestock out to graze in the delicately beautiful, flower-filled meadows of the valley.

In order to avoid such problems and to make the valley reasonably accessible to the public, Olmsted called for a state appropriation of $25,000 to construct an access road. Another $12,000 would be required over the following two years, he said, to cover the cost of survey work involved in the transfer of the Yosemite and Mariposa Big Tree Grove from federal to state jurisdiction, for construction of roads, trails, and other visitor facilities in the valley, and to cover the $1,200 salary of a superintendent.

Olmsted's report was apparently received with enthusiasm by the commission members and visitors who were present that day. Ironically, however,

the commission did not officially adopt Olmsted's report either then or later. Thus it was never presented to the state legislature or to the governor, who was ex-officio chairman of the commission. Inside opinion held that J. D. Whitney suppressed the report in order to keep its rather large budget request from competing for the state funds he needed to conduct the California Geological Survey.

Olmsted himself was not around to argue the matter. He left California in October 1865 in order to return to work on Central Park in New York City, and to begin work on Prospect Park, another large "rural park" in Brooklyn. With his departure the Yosemite Commission lapsed into nearly complete inactivity, and despite steadily growing national and international fame as a scenic attraction, the "state park" at Yosemite and the Mariposa Grove of Big Trees entered a prolonged period of neglect, political wrangling, and bitter controversy.

The trouble stemmed partly from a lack of interest and professional judgment on the part of the commission, and partly from the determined and

energetic opposition of one man, James Mason Hutchings.

The Hutchings Dispute

James Mason Hutchings had come to California in the gold rush of 1849 and thrown himself into mining, then banking, then publishing, and finally—in 1864—into hotel-keeping in Yosemite Valley. Hutching's California Magazine (1856-61) had made its editor-publisher famous though not particularly prosperous. Hotel-keeping in Yosemite Valley on the other hand, looked to him like an enjoyable and profitable way to cash in on his fame as an interpreter of the California scene. After 1864 he continued to build a public following through lecture tours, and published promotional materials about Yosemite, the Sierra Nevada, and, of course, his hotel. Because of his reputation, and the fact that many visitors to his hotel were prosperous and highly influential, Hutchings could be a formidable opponent in political matters, particularly on the state level.

The terms of the federal grant accepted by the state in April 1866 ex-

"Yosemite Domes," photo by Carleton E. Watkins.

pressly prohibited private claims to land in Yosemite Valley, but Hutchings maintained that he and at least one other settler had established "possessory interest" in their Yosemite properties prior to approval of the federal legislation. He also maintained that the Yosemite Commission had no power to regulate his use of his property, or to evict him, or to do anything not specifically authorized by the legislature. The state legislature obviously agreed with him, for they passed a resolution—over the governor's veto—asking Congress to redraw the boundaries of the Yosemite grant in such a way as to recognize the private claims! Congress refused to do so, however, and soon afterward the Yosemite Commission began eviction proceedings.

Throughout the prolonged legal and political struggle that ensued, Hutchings compaigned for public sympathy both in California and across the nation. In 1872, however, the U.S. Supreme Court upheld a California Supreme Court decision that Hutchings' claim was invalid. The high court also decreed that the California legislature had no legal right to interfere with or dictate Yosemite Commission administrative policies. "The public, or the people for whom the state holds the grant in trust," said California Supreme Court Justice John Currey, "are not the people of California alone, but all the people of the United States and perhaps

of the world, who may choose to avail themselves of the use of the property granted for resort and recreation."

Meanwhile, as long as the controversy and litigation continued, the state legislature refused to appropriate *any* money for the development or even the management and protection of Yosemite.

In 1866 the Yosemite Commission had adopted a set of management regulations, and had appointed one of its members, Galen Clark, to be the "Guardian" of Yosemite—in effect, the first California state park ranger. Clark's salary was very small; he and the "sub-Guardian" were to share $500 per year. But Clark was in love with the Big Trees and with Yosemite, and therefore considered it an honor and a privilege to hold the appointment. One measure of his dedication is that he continued on the job—greeting, advising and guiding visitors, enforcing regulations, cleaning up, building and repairing bridges and trails, even paying the "sub-Guardian" out of his own pocket —even though his own pay was held up for a full six years! Moreover, by all accounts, he carried out these tasks with energy, enthusiasm, ingenuity, and determination as well as unfailing tact and courtesy.

In 1874, despite the Supreme Court decision against Hutchings, the state legislature appropriated $60,000 with which to buy up all of the private claims

in Yosemite Valley. Hutchings received $24,000 for his hotel property, and then refused to either move out or apply for a lease on the property from the commission. Finally, the sheriff of Mariposa County, and Galen Clark as deputy sheriff, had to evict him.

Management by Concession

Once the Hutchings dispute was resolved, the legislature was somewhat more generous in its appropriations on behalf of Yosemite. Nevertheless, public opinion with regard to Yosemite Commission management policies continued mixed. Everyone agreed that the natural scenery was magnificent, and that a trip to the area was worthwhile despite its many aggravations. But as visitation continued to increase, the inadequacy of the roads and other facilities became ever more evident. Since the state had not provided money for the construction of access roads, the Yosemite Commission had resorted to encouraging private construction of toll roads. The irony of that policy, of course, was that soon the public land in Yosemite could hardly be visited at all except by paying a fee and otherwise obtaining permission from private parties to cross private land on privately owned toll roads. And the roads themselves—built for profit and not under public jurisdiction—were often in

Stoneman House and Stoneman "meadow" about 1890. The much-criticized hotel was destroyed by fire in 1896.

poor condition despite stiff toll charges.

This problem was only slightly altered in the late 1870s when an access road suitable for wagons was completed all the way into the valley, and when the state appropriated just enough money to acquire the portion of the access road that lay inside the park boundary.

The Yosemite Commission, meanwhile, had also been granting special concessions to private parties in order to get them to provide supplies and build trails and hotel facilities in the valley itself. Along with various management problems, this policy eventually led to charges of political favoritism and mismanagement. In 1880, as a result of such charges, the legislature declared all of the commission seats vacant, and asked Governor George C. Perkins to select new commissioners. If possible, the governor was to choose a majority of the new commissioners from among persons "resident in the counties most affected by the actions of said Commission." The legislature also increased the salary of the guardian to $1,500 per year.

In April 1880 the governor appointed new commissioners. They in turn fired Galen Clark from his position as guardian and replaced him with none other than James M. Hutchings. The legality of these changes was contested in court by members of the old commission. But the issues involved were not simple. The case went all the way to the U.S. Supreme Court before a final decision favoring the governor and the new commission was finally rendered in March 1881. Meanwhile, the guardian and the old commission refused to admit that they had been replaced.

Despite the cloud under which their tenure began, the new commission and the new guardian went about their responsibilities with enthusiasm and high hopes. Concerned about unregulated sheep grazing, tree cutting, and use of fire in the watershed above Yosemite Valley itself, the commission appealed to Congress, the Secretary of Interior, and to President Garfield to enlarge the Yosemite grant to include the whole Merced River watershed. Congressional legislation was submitted. But President Garfield was assassinated in September 1881, and without his support the legislation died quietly in committee.

The commission suffered another setback early in the 1880s when legislation calling for a $25,000 appropriation for Yosemite improvements was vetoed by the governor. They pressed onward, however, and in 1884 persuaded a new governor, George Stoneman, to attend the June meeting of the commission in Yosemite Valley. In 1885 the legislature appropriated $40,000 for a new hotel, plus $20,000 for hotel furnishings and the development of a water supply. Grateful for this unprecedented state support of Yosemite development efforts, the commission promptly named the new hotel (completed in 1887) in honor of Governor Stoneman.

The Yosemite Commission looked upon "Stoneman House" as hard evidence that the legislature and the governor were willing at last to support proper development of the valley. Commission critics, however, considered the hotel ugly and poorly located—just one more example of the commission's inability to manage the federal grant.

According to Olmsted and others including Robert Underwood Johnson, editor of *Century Magazine,* the trouble was that the commissioners were all businessmen and politicians rather than artists, landscape architects, or park managers. They simply did not have the training and background that were necessary to take proper care of Yosemite. "They may think it more desirable," Johnson said, "to improve a trail than to preserve the sentiment for which the trail exists." Already the commission had allowed the flower-filled meadows of the valley to be plowed up and turned into pasture land and corrals for livestock. This policy not only destroyed the natural beauty of the meadows, but as Johnson and others pointed out, it also resulted in the stringing of barbed-wire fences that made it difficult for park visitors to explore the valley.

Lacking expert advice about park values, and continually beset by provincial, personal, political, and commercial considerations, the commission was *likely* to do the wrong thing. Even when the commissioners did seek expert advice they tended to select people with little or no sensitivity to the intrinsic but subtle value of undisturbed wilderness. One professor of electrical engineering, for example, called for construction of a generating plant that would make it possible to illuminate the cliffs at night with powerful beams of colored light. William Hammond Hall, the state engineer in 1885, concluded that some valley floor meadow areas were being used "inefficiently." He recommended that they *all* be fenced and plowed. Hall had done wonderful work on the man-made environment of Golden Gate Park in San Francisco, but apparently he was unimpressed by the natural beauty of Yosemite's meadowlands.

Critics of the Yosemite Commission were not pleased by the prospect that commission control might be extended to the whole Merced River watershed. They argued that the federal government should retain title to the watershed as a whole, and that Yosemite Valley should also be put beyond the reach of local politics and commercial interests. The whole area, they said, should be administered as a national park. "It is to the interest of the valley, the commissioners, the state, the nation, and the world," said Robert Underwood Johnson, "that California should adopt an intelligent and generous policy towards the Yosemite with a view to placing it in skillful hands and devising a permanent plan which shall take it, once for all, out of the reach of the dangers by which it is now seriously threatened."

The most appealing and persuasive spokesman for this point of view during the 1880s and '90s was John Muir, who had been closely associated with Yosemite Valley and the Mariposa Grove of Big Trees since his arrival in California in 1868. To support himself during his first years in Yosemite he had worked as sheepherder, sawyer, and carpenter. During this time, he was, as he called himself, "an unknown nobody in the woods". But whatever he called himself, Muir was above all else

John Muir in 1872.

an extraordinarily intense and gifted student of nature. Before long he was in great demand as tour guide and interpreter of the unique natural features of the Yosemite region. Starting as early as 1871, some of the world's leading scientists, artists, writers, and philosophers including Asa Gray, George Tyndall, and Ralph Waldo Emerson, sought him out in the valley in order to confer with him and encourage him to continue his lonely, carefully detailed, and at times highly controversial studies of glacial activity and other natural phenomena.

Soon Muir found that he could support himself as writer and lecturer on the subjects that interested him most. Within a few years he was nationally recognized and celebrated both as a scientific observer of nature and as a popular writer—a leading spokesman for the wilderness and for the healing and restorative value of wilderness experience.

Muir had long been critical of the way development was being allowed to proceed in Yosemite Valley. He bitterly resented the "vulgar, mercenary 'improvement' " that was destroying the natural beauty and spontaneity of the valley's delicate "wild gardens." He took comfort only in the fact that things were not worse than they were, and that "the moneychangers" would not be able to "improve" Yosemite's massive walls and domes and waterfalls.

Yosemite events during the 1880s persuaded many people that Muir and other critics were correct—that something was basically wrong with Yosemite management policy. Hutchings' tenure as guardian (1880-84) was marked by increasingly angry charges of collusion and mismanagement to the undue benefit of the hotel keepers and transportation companies serving Yosemite. In 1884 Hutchings was replaced by Walter E. Dennison, a mining and transportation company official. And Dennison in turn was replaced in 1887 by Mark L. McCord, a Southern Pacific Railroad employee. Neither of these men had any park management experience or any special knowledge of Yosemite conditions.

Controversy over Yosemite management policies rose to new heights in 1888 when Charles D. Robinson, a well-known painter and photographer from San Francisco, took his complaints to the press and backed up some of his more specific charges with highly persuasive photographic evidence. In February 1889 the California State Senate decided to investigate. Witnesses were called, charges and countercharges were leveled, but the result—including 430 pages of transcript—was inconclusive. Galen Clark said that he blamed none of his successors. In his quiet way he simply recommended that Yosemite not be run for profit.

The final result of the senate investigation was an official statement completely exonerating the Yosemite Commission. At roughly the same time, however, in June 1889, Galen Clark was appointed guardian once again, and told to proceed with many of the improvements and reforms that he felt were important. Clark was now 75 years old, but with the full support of the commission and the press, he set to work with enthusiasm.

In this photo by Carleton E. Watkins (late 1850s or early 1860s), Galen Clark stands at the foot of the Grizzly Giant in the Mariposa Grove in his rough frontier clothing, his long rifle in one hand and a sprig of giant sequoia foliage in the other.

The National Park at Yosemite

The Yosemite Commission and the state legislature in 1889 agreed to pursue enlargement of the federal grant at Yosemite, but California representatives in Washington, D.C. soon found that eastern sentiment was swinging away from the idea of continued state control of the valley. Legislation providing for enlargement of the grant was supplanted by another bill passed on September 30, 1890 that called for the creation of a 932,600 acre "forest reserve" surrounding Yosemite Valley. This new "reserve" was to be administered not by the State of California, but by the federal government acting through the Secretary of the Interior. Boundaries of the "reserve" were virtually identical to the "national park" boundaries proposed by John Muir in correspondence with Robert Underwood Johnson, and in two articles by Muir that appeared in Johnson's *Century Magazine* in August and September while Congress was considering the Yosemite question. These two articles, "Treasures of the Yosemite" and "Features of the Pro-

posed Yosemite National Park," were extremely popular, widely reprinted, and no doubt helped set the proper atmosphere for passage of the federal legislation.

Muir and other insiders, however, were quick to give credit to the Southern Pacific Railroad's Washington lobbyists for the sudden success of the congressional legislation that created forest reserves not only at Yosemite, but also in the areas known as Sequoia and General Grant National Parks in the southern Sierra. Southern Pacific, it seems, was strongly interested in the development of tourism in the Far West.

After President Benjamin Harrison signed this legislation on October 1, 1890, it was up to John W. Noble, the Secretary of Interior, to determine a management policy for the new "forest reserve" at Yosemite. An enthusiastic reader of Muir's articles and a ready advocate of wilderness preservation, Noble unhesitatingly indicated that the new "reserve" should be administered as a "public park." And since the legislation empowered the Secretary of Interior to name the new "reserve," Noble promptly decreed that it should hence-

forth be known as Yosemite National Park. Early in 1891 a troop of federal cavalry was dispatched to begin regular patrols.

In 1892 a group of San Francisco-based business and professional men got together with some academicians from Stanford and the University of California to form the Sierra Club. Their objective was to provide a popular base of support for the protection of the new Yosemite National Park. They were concerned first of all that Congress might decide to revise the park boundaries or even abandon the park entirely. More specifically they were concerned about the possibility of physical invasion of the park by livestock, mining, and lumbering interests. Even with John Muir as president, however, the club as a whole was reluctant to enter the controversy over management problems in the valley itself. Instead, at least for the first few years, club leaders tried to conciliate and work cooperatively with the Yosemite Commission.

Meanwhile, following his reappointment as guardian in June 1889, Galen Clark was trying diligently to improve conditions in Yosemite Valley. He re-

moved some of the offensive pasture fences, and improved trails and other visitor facilities. He cleared brush away from the edges of Mirror Lake in order to restore its reflective quality—so highly admired in earlier years. He handled complaints and problems of all kinds with unwavering diplomacy and firmness. Fully aware of the age-old Indian policy of periodic burning, Clark also tried to persuade the commission that an ongoing program of brush removal and tree thinning would have to be conducted if the forest and meadows were to remain open and "park-like." An almost entirely new commission appointed by Governor Waterman in 1890 approved Clark's brush and tree removal program, and some work of the kind was accomplished during 1891 and 1892. Shortly afterward, however, public controversy brought the program to a halt.

Despite all of the well-intentioned efforts of Clark and others, criticism of the commission and of conditions in Yosemite Valley continued and even increased during the 1890s. Secretary of the Interior John Noble charged, for instance, that state control of the valley had resulted in undue "destruction of timber, some for buildings, fences and fuel; some removed simply for cultivation, and a great deal laid waste through carelessness and wantonness; that more than half the valley had been fenced with barbed wire fencing, and cultivated with grasses and grain; that these enclosures have confined travel to narrow limits between fences and the slopes of the mountains, and have left but little room for paths for pedestrians up the valley; that a great many rare plants new to botany have been destroyed by plowing and pasturing the valley; that management has fallen into the hands of a monopoly, and no competition seems to be permitted in hotel accommodations, transportation, or furnishing of provender for the animals of tourists." These and other "acts of spoilation and trespass have been per-

mitted for a number of years, and seem to have become a part of the settled policy of the management."

In its own defense, the Yosemite Commission charged that the federal government was delinquent in not providing money for public acquisition of the privately owned toll roads that led to Yosemite. The commission also charged that "except for a patrol of soldiers it [the federal government] has utterly neglected this park reservation. In contrast with this is its policy to the Yellowstone, where about a million dollars have been spent, and the Chattanooga National Park, where over a million dollars have been expended."

The result of all this high level attention was a standoff. One solution, proposed more and more frequently, was that Yosemite Valley should be given back to the federal government. But at least during the early 1890s, neither Congress nor the State of California was ready to seriously consider such a course of action. Support for "recession" nevertheless continued to accumulate.

After his retirement in 1896 at the age of 82, even Galen Clark came to believe that Yosemite Valley would be better managed by the federal government. The trouble with state management of the valley, as both he and John Muir agreed, was that political and profit-oriented considerations too often interfered with the long-term best inerests of the park and park visitors. Management of the valley, as Muir put it, should ideally "be taken wholly out of the Governor's hands. The office changes too often and must always be more or less mixed with politics in its bearing upon appointments for the valley." They agreed that the valley could best be administered by a smaller, more professional, perhaps even paid commission whose members would serve longer terms. Since creation of this kind of commission did not seem to be politically feasible through state action, Muir, Clark, and an increasing

number of other students of Yosemite came to support federal management of the valley.

Despite Muir's well-known opinions on the matter, the Sierra Club continued to strive for good working relations with the Yosemite Commission. There were many reasons for this. For one thing, strong ties of personal friendship existed between members of the club and members of the commission. The San Francisco attorney, Warren Olney, for example, played a leading role in the club throughout its early years and at the same time was a close personal friend of John P. Irish, chairman of the Yosemite Commission from 1889 to 1893. In the heated arguments over Yosemite expansion in 1890, Irish had gone beyond the issues to publicly attack Muir's personal honesty and integrity. This kind of animosity must have caused Olney and other club leaders considerable anguish, but they remained confident that the club itself should continue to avoid conflict with the commission.

During the middle 1890s, therefore, the Sierra Club functioned very much in the way that cooperating associations and citizen advisory groups function today in relation to state and national parks. The club advised the commission on various administrative questions, and lobbied on behalf of the park. And club members became actively involved in park interpretation—working on trails, building a monument at Glacier Point complete with an index to the famous panoramic view, and in 1898 establishing a visitor center with an "alpine library" and an attendant who would assist the guardian "by directing campers to their grounds" and providing "information for travel into the wonders of these peaks, volcanoes of the past, glaciers, rivers, and lakes."

The first person selected to represent the club in Yosemite was an enthusiastic young student of wilderness and the Sierra Nevada high country by the name of William E. Colby. A dedicated ama-

Theodore Roosevelt and John Muir in the Mariposa Grove, May 1903. Others in the groups, right to left: *Benjamin Ide Wheeler (President of the University of California), private secretary Loeb, Nicholas Murray Butler (President of Columbia University), Muir, Dr. Rixey, President Roosevelt, Governor Pardee, Secretary of the Navy Moody, and Secret Service men.*

teur naturalist who had known and admired John Muir since childhood, Will Colby had just finished law school and was soon to join the law faculty at the University of California. Along with a distinguished career in mining law, Colby would also go on to play a central role in Sierra Club, mountaineering, environmental, and California park matters over the next 50 years and more.

In 1896 and 1897 Warren Olney and other Sierra Club leaders began to agree with Muir that recession was the best policy for Yosemite Valley. But not until the turn of the century was Muir (with Colby's help) able to persuade the club to actively campaign for recession. And not until the club was enthusiastically behind him was Muir able to make significant progress toward that goal.

The Campaign for Recession

In 1903 an important opportunity to lobby for recession was offered to Muir in the form of an invitation to accompany President Theodore Roosevelt on a trip to Yosemite. Muir, however, was reluctant. He had corresponded with the president on forestry matters and they were on good terms, but the trip conflicted with arrangements he had already made for a world tour with his old friend Charles Sargent, the eminent Harvard botanist. When the president learned of Muir's previous commitment, he immediately wrote Muir urging him to take time for the Yosemite trip: "I do not want anyone with me but you, and I want to drop politics absolutely for four days, and just be out in the open with you."

On May 14, 1903 Muir joined the presidential party in San Francisco and traveled with the president up into the mountains. Repeatedly avoiding the hotel accommodations, banquets, celebrations, and special events planned for the president by the Yosemite Commission and others, Roosevelt and Muir spent three days on the trail together, camping out under the stars, and talking about forest preservation, Yosemite, and related matters. The president was delighted with the whole experience, commenting at one point that "This has been the grandest day of my life! One I shall long remember!" Later both he and California Governor

George C. Pardee let it be known that they were committed to recession.

With the president and the governor on record in favor of recession, an increasing number of other Republican politicians also came to favor it. The tide was turning, but there were still many who felt that giving the Yosemite grant back to the federal government would be insulting and degrading to California, an admission that California could not properly care for such a natural treasure.

Despite this argument, an increasing number of professional and citizen groups including the California Press Association, the California Water and Forest Association, the Sempervirens Club, and the Native Sons of the Golden West, began to favor recession. Their arguments were basically the same: overlap of authority and jurisdiction in Yosemite was inefficient and led to troublesome administrative conflicts; the legislature had provided insufficient money to improve park roads and other facilities; federal control of the valley would constitute no loss at all to California, either in practical terms or by way of prestige.

In 1904 the California Board of Trade published a diplomatic but very telling report, pointing out that "the gentlemen appointed from time to time to this important office [the Yosemite Commission] have been selected from among our best citizens, men of culture, refinement and education, who are lovers of nature and deeply interested in the development of the State. . . . Every report made by these commissioners since the beginning, recites to what degree and extent they are hampered by the lack of funds to carry on much needed improvements and provide for the steadily increasing influx of tourist travel." Some legislatures, the report said, had been reasonably generous, though most had not, and always the appropriations had been "inadequate to fulfill the demand."

The report also pointed out that the state legislature had spent $495,000 on Yosemite over a period of 40 years, whereas in 25 years the federal government had spent $1.5 million on Yellowstone. As a result, the Yellowstone park which was younger and far more remote from any center of population, had nearly twice as many visit-

ors as Yosemite. The report closed with a description of how important tourism was to the Swiss economy and how much money might come into California through tourism if Yosemite were made easily accessible. With all this in mind, the report concluded, trade associations in every county were enthusiastically adopting resolutions favoring recession.

In January 1905 a recession bill was introduced in the California legislature. Drafted by Colby at Muir's request and actively supported in Sacramento by both men, the bill ran into heated opposition. Despite widespread support built up by years of preparation, and even with active support from the Board of Trade and the powerful Southern Pacific Railroad lobby, the bill squeaked through the state senate by just one vote.

But the struggle was not yet over. Federal acceptance of the valley also required congressional approval. And when the matter was taken up by Congress, many objections were raised. Boundary revisions were proposed. Fiscal problems were cited. Grazing and lumbering interests were especially outspoken in their arguments against the bill. Nevertheless, with crucial behind-the-scenes support from the Southern Pacific Railroad Company, a bill calling for recession was passed by Congress and signed by President Roosevelt on June 11, 1906. After 42 years as a state park, Yosemite Valley and the Mariposa Grove of Big Trees were at last integral parts of Yosemite National Park.

Of course, those who hoped that national park status would stop all controversy and completely protect wilderness values within the park were soon to be disillusioned. Inholdings by mining, grazing, and lumbering interests continued to be a problem, and the great Hetch Hetchy controversy was already brewing.

In 1907, however, completion of the Yosemite Railroad from Merced to El Portal began to make a reality of Olmsted's dream that everyone, not just the rich and privileged few, could visit the incredibly beautiful wilderness area the nation had set aside in the midst of civil war "for public use, resort and recreation" forevermore—"inalienable for all time."

2 California Redwood Park

"The coast redwood forests of California are being swiftly and surely destroyed by the remorseless needs of improvement. And I recognize both the futility and the injustice of attempting to ignore or to resist these needs. Yet I insist upon the perfect justice of taking all lawful means to save forever some portion of these matchless forests.

Ralph Sidney Smith, 1887

Left: *The Compass Group at Big Basin. Photo by Andrew P. Hill.* Below: *Andrew P. Hill circa 1900.*

While the campaign was still underway to return Yosemite Valley and the Mariposa Grove to federal control, the State of California took steps to create a new state park deep in the heart of the rugged, heavily forested Santa Cruz Mountains. The new park was in an area long known as the "Big Basin," and featured an exceptionally grand forest of *Sequoia sempervirens,* or coast redwoods.

People had been talking about the desirability of preserving a portion of the great coast redwood forest for many years. As early as 1852, Assemblyman Henry A. Crabb asked the legislature to maintain all of the state's redwood forest lands in public ownership. In 1879, Carl Shurz, Secretary of the Interior under President Rutherford B. Hayes, asked Congress to set aside a coast redwood preserve of at least two townships—46,080 acres. And there were many other redwood preservation proposals made by various individuals, official and unofficial, over the years. But none of these proposals was reinforced by evidence of widespread and persistent public support.

The idea of a park that would preserve the primeval redwood forest of Big Basin was first brought to life during the 1880s by the eloquence of Ralph Sidney Smith, the brilliant young editor and manager of the *Redwood City Times and Gazette.* A native of San Mateo County, Smith had known the Santa Cruz Mountain forests from childhood. His enthusiasm for the area was infectious, and his position as editor of the *Times and Gazette* gave him an excellent opportunity to shape public opinion. In 1886 he started writing about the wisdom of preserving a portion of California's unique redwood forest not only as a tourist attraction of economic importance, but also for scientific purposes, and as a long-term investment in the education and inspiration of present and future generations.

Logging activities were rapidly invading the area, but it was still possible, Smith said, to acquire an outstanding example of virgin redwood forest in the Santa Cruz Mountains south of San Francisco. He focused his attention at first on the great forest that still stood in the upper portions of the Pescadero and Butano Creek watersheds. Here, a 20,000-acre redwood park could be acquired for no more than $15 an acre. Smith personally promised to raise half of the acquisition costs from private sources if the state would "appropriate a reasonably generous sum" with which to start the acquisition process.

His proposal was enthusiastically endorsed by many San Francisco Bay Area newspapers. It was also favorably commented on by ex-Governor Leland Stanford, then serving in the U.S. Senate, by William H. Jordan, Speaker of the State Assembly, and by many other public figures and leading journalists including Ambrose Bierce, and the poet Joaquin Miller. Despite this sudden wave of interest, the 27th Legislature adjourned April 12, 1887 without taking action on the proposed park.

Smith did not give up, however. He turned his attention to the possibility of immediate private acquisition of a suitable area that the state could acquire for park purposes at a later time. Even though legislative inaction in 1887 meant that it was too late to save the ancient redwoods of Pescadero and Butano creeks, there was still time to do something just to the south in the "Big Basin" where an exceptionally fine forest was still available at a reasonable price. In April 1887 Smith arranged a special expedition to Big Basin for the benefit of journalists and "representative men" of the day. He also began to plan his strategy for the next session of the legislature, which was scheduled to convene in January 1889. Then, suddenly, the campaign came to a complete stop.

On November 29, 1887 Ralph Sidney Smith was shot in the back and killed by a man whose business ethics Smith had criticized in print. Smith died of his wounds on November 30, and with him the campaign for a state park in the Santa Cruz Mountains also died—at least for the time being.

Over the next decade and more, various articles about the coast redwoods and about the desirability of preserving some of them from logging appeared from time to time in newspapers, magazines and books both locally and internationally. But there was no organization, and no leader, to give this widespread interest a focal point. In 1890 the federal government created Sequoia, General Grant, and Yosemite national parks partly in order

The gathering at Stanford University, May 1, 1900. Left to right: *J. H. Senger, David Starr Jordan, W. R. Dudley, F. W. Billings, James McNaughton, J. Q. Packard, William T. Jeter, John E. Richards, Carrie Stevens Walter, J. M. Stillman, Charles B. Wing, John J. Montgomery, R. L. Green. Photo by Andrew P. Hill.*

to protect *Sequoiadendron giganteum,* the Sierra redwood, from logging. But as the years went by no similar action was taken by any level of government to give park status to any portion of the coast redwood forest.

In September 1899 a gifted painter and photographer by the name of Andrew P. Hill accepted a photographic assignment from *Wide World,* an English magazine which was planning to publish an article about redwoods. In order to obtain the desired photographs Hill took the train, which then ran between San Jose and Santa Cruz, and stopped off, camera in hand, at the Felton Grove. The grove, now part of Henry Cowell Redwoods State Park, was then privately owned and operated as a tourist attraction complete with admission fee and hotel facilities. Hill paid his fee, took his photographs, and then decided to look up the owner of the grove in order to ask some historical questions.

According to Hill, the owner of the grove "was very much disturbed to learn that I had photographed the trees and told me that no photographs of them were allowed to be taken by an outsider, as they were the perquisites of the hotel." Hill tried to persuade the hotel owner that publication of the photographs would be good publicity, but the man was not mollified, refused to answer any historical questions, and demanded that Hill surrender his newly exposed photographic plates. Hill refused, and left the grove to catch the train back to San Jose.

Waiting for the train, Hill had time to think about what had just happened. "I was a little angry, and somewhat disgusted. . . . The thought flashed through my mind that these trees, because of their size and antiquity, were among the natural wonders of the world, and should be saved for posterity. I said to myself, 'I will start a campaign immediately to make a public park of this place.' "

Andrew Hill was an idealist, and a man of extraordinary energy and determination. His circle of friends was broad, and through his work he was in touch with many popular writers of the day. His optimism and irrepressibly cheerful manner made him hard to resist. Before he even reached San Jose he met one of his writer friends on the

train and persuaded him to do a redwood article for the *San Jose Herald.* At a way-station he left a note for Josephine Clifford McCrackin, another locally well-known writer, asking her to do a similar article for the *Santa Cruz Sentinel.* Both of these articles were written and published and then widely reprinted in newspapers throughout California. Soon other writers also took up the cause and thus, almost overnight, a serious campaign got underway.

Though he could ill afford to take so much time away from his artistic and commercial affairs, Hill threw himself into a whirlwind series of lectures before chambers of commerce, service clubs, women's clubs, the Native Sons and Daughters of the Golden West, academic groups, and anyone else who was interested and might be able to help. Many of these groups adopted resolutions calling for Congress to create a Santa Cruz Mountains redwood national park that would include the Felton Grove.

In April 1900 the campaign took a new turn. Hill was asked to call a public meeting of potential park supporters. He decided it was crucial for a park campaign to be completely non-partisan, and that the best way to launch such a campaign was to rely upon the prestige and leadership of the foremost educational institutions of the day.

David Starr Jordan, president of Stanford University, agreed with Hill and offered to host the meeting.

On May 1, 1900, in the library at Stanford, a well-publicized meeting of influential citizens was held, and a decision was made to focus not on the Felton Grove but on the much larger, more spectacular, and more completely untouched redwood forest in Big Basin. This decision was based in large part on second-hand information, though several members of the group were personally familiar with Big Basin. Botany professor William R. Dudley, for example, had explored the area and had proposed in 1895 that Stanford University acquire the basin as a scientific preserve. Colonel Wing, a professor of civil engineering, had accompanied Dudley and mapped the area. Their descriptions of Big Basin were so intriguing that several members of the group immediately began to plan a field trip.

On the fifteenth of May, Hill and four others started for Big Basin. They were met at Boulder Creek by members of the Santa Cruz Chamber of Commerce, and by H. L. Middleton, agent for the lumber company that held options on most of the basin. The next evening they were joined in the basin itself by Charles Wesley Reed, a member of the San Francisco Board of Supervisors. For the next three days the group ex-

In Big Basin, May 1900. Left to right: *Louise C. Jones, Carrie Stevens Walter, J. F. Coope, J. Q. Packard, Andy Baldwin, Charles Wesley Reed, W. W. Richards, Roley Kooser. Photo By Andrew P. Hill.*

plored the entire area with steadily rising enthusiasm, searching out the many waterfalls and wandering awe-struck through Big Basin's major redwood groves.

On the evening of May 18, on the west bank of Sempervirens Creek opposite Slippery Rock, the group decided to form a permanent organization dedicated to preserving the natural environment of Big Basin as a public park. Officers were chosen, a hat was passed and $32 collected, and the new organization was named—the Sempervirens Club.

Membership in the new club was soon expanded to include representatives of Stanford University, Santa Clara University, California State Normal School (now San Jose State University), the University of California at Berkeley, various chambers of commerce, women's clubs, and other citizen organizations including the Sierra Club. Some members of the new club were already hard at work on behalf of national park status for the world famous Calaveras Grove of Big Trees which had recently been purchased by a lumber company. On the advice of the congressman who was handling the Calaveras Big Trees matter, the Sempervirens Club decided to shift its strategy and strive for the creation of a state park at Big Basin. Thus, the campaign that Ralph Sidney Smith had begun so

many years earlier was fully resurrected and infused with new energy. Nor was Smith himself forgotten in this movement, for his name was often mentioned throughout the campaign that followed.

During the summer and autumn months, meetings were held and a fund-raising campaign was launched— Phoebe Apperson Hearst was particularly generous in this regard—and in January 1901 a bill was introduced in the state assembly by George H. Fisk of San Francisco. Drafted by Charles Reed, who was then serving as president of the Sempervirens Club, the bill called for the creation of a California Redwood Park Commission made up of the governor and four other commissioners to be appointed by the governor. This group would select a suitable redwood forest park site, which would then be acquired "for the honor of California and the benefit of succeeding generations." The bill set a maximum acquisition price of $500,000 and called for the immediate appropriation of half that sum.

The bill immediately ran into trouble in both houses of the legislature, and was written off as hopelessly dead by knowledgeable observers. Among park supporters only Andrew Hill refused to give up. As a delegation of one, Hill promptly left for Sacramento where he conferred with the very popular young assemblyman Alden Anderson who, like

Hill, had strong ties to people in San Jose. Anderson (Assembly Speaker, 1899; and Lieutenant Governor, 1903-07) suggested that the total appropriation for acquisition be cut to $250,000 and that actual expenditure of the funds be spread out over five years at $50,000 per year. He also advised Hill to seek the help of Sacramento Assemblyman Grove L. Johnson, a veteran legislator and a leader of the Southern Pacific Railroad Company's political machine in the state legislature. Hill showed Johnson his Big Basin photographs, and described the area and the popular movement for its preservation. Soon afterward, with Johnson's help, the park legislation was out of committee and moving once again.

In order to get the bill through the legislature, however, still more support was thought to be needed. And so, over the next two months, Hill and the Sempervirens Club made a concerted drive to demonstrate statewide interest and support. Newspaper and magazine stories were written and sent out. Leaflets were published. Key people were identified and interviewed. Special field trips to Big Basin were conducted by Hill and others. Women's clubs throughout the state were especially active, and through the influence of Reverend Robert E. Kenna, president of Santa Clara University, the Society of Jesuits and Catholic church members

California Redwood Park Commission and Advisory Board in Big Basin, September 1901. Seated, left to right: *W. R. Dudley, Hervey Lindley, W. H. Mills, Governor Henry Gage.* Standing behind the governor: *Rev. Robert E. Kenna.*

Main entrance gate,
California Redwood Park.

Big Basin ranger and jack-of-all trades, circa 1910.

from many parts of the state also became actively involved. As a result, when the Big Basin bill finally came to a vote early in March, it was given almost unanimous approval by both houses of the legislature.

The signature of Governor Henry T. Gage was still needed, however, to make the bill effective. And the governor announced himself to be in a quandry because the legislature had also approved a bill calling for the creation of a statewide forest and water conservation commission. Pledged as he was to economy in government, Gage felt that he could not sign both bills. On March 16, however, after conferring with David Starr Jordan, and after another public hearing and another outpouring of public support from individuals and groups throughout the state, the governor signed the Big Basin legislation and decided to let the forest and water conservation bill die.

The California Redwood Park Commission appointed by Governor Gage included two academicians: Professor William R. Dudley, chairman of the botany department at Stanford University, and Reverend Robert E. Kenna of Santa Clara University. Gage also appointed two railroad men: A. W. Foster of the Northern Pacific, also a regent of the University of California; and William H. Mills, land agent for the Southern Pacific. Mills had been one of the leading supporters of the forest and water conservation bill, and was so disgusted by the governor's veto of that legislation that he was now quite surprised to find himself on the park commission. It may well be, therefore, that Mills tried to block acquisition of land in Big Basin for reasons of revenge. Whatever his motives, however, it is a fact that he raised one objection after another, and publicized his opinion that Big Basin was too remote for park purposes, and that land in the area was overpriced.

The prolonged delay brought about by Mills' opposition caused considerable agony for the Sempervirens Club and H. L. Middleton of the Big Basin Land and Lumber Company. Middleton was an enthusiastic supporter of the park concept, but his company was in the lumber business, and as of November 1900 had already made plans and brought in machinery to start logging operations in Big Basin. In order to

Andrew P. Hill and the Sempervirens Club seated at the base of the Father of the Forest, Big Basin circa 1915.

forestall that logging, Middleton and the Sempervirens Club negotiated one option after another pending a decision about the park. To their lasting credit, Middleton and his company remained patient and cooperative despite the many delays. At last, in September 1902, after exhaustive testimony as to the value of the land and timber in Big Basin, and after a personal inspection by the governor, the commission agreed to acquire 2,500 acres in Big Basin at $100 an acre. An additional 1,300 acres of brush and cut-over lands were then donated to the park by the Big Basin Land and Lumber Company, and later, still other private lands were donated to the state by Middleton and others in order to help round out the park. Another significant addition was accomplished in 1908 when the Sempervirens Club and the park commission succeeded in having 3,980 acres of federal lands in Big Basin turned over to the state for inclusion in the park, thus bringing about half of the Waddell Creek watershed inside the park boundaries. The Sempervirens Club believed that the park should include the whole watershed, but many years would pass before that dream would approach reality.

On July 1, 1903, Mr. J. H. B. Pilkington, Horticultural Commissioner of Santa Cruz County, was chosen to superintend the new state park. As "Park Warden" it was his job to protect the park from misuse, and to expend the $10,000 appropriated by the legislature for development of the area. Under his leadership the park officially opened to camping and other public uses on June 1, 1904. That season was hardly over, however, when disaster struck.

Early in September during a tremendous heat wave, a fire started in the sawdust pile at Waterman's lumber mill north of the park. Driven by a hot dry wind, the fire raced southwesterly over the ridges and into the park, running all the way to the sea in some places. Warden Pilkington and a crew of up to 100 men managed to protect the central part of the park, but only cool weather and a rainstorm completely killed the fire — 20 days after it had begun.

In 1905 Governor George C. Pardee and the state legislature disbanded the Redwood Park Commission and re-

placed it with a new commission made up of the governor, secretary of state, attorney general, secretary of the Board of Examiners, and the state forester. In actual practice, this meant that the state forester was in charge of Big Basin, a state of affairs that probably pleased the governor who was an enthusiastic supporter of the U. S. Forest Service and its founder, Gifford Pinchot. Like Pinchot, the governor favored forest "conservation" as opposed to total, park-style "preservation." According to the Pinchot school of thought, conservation meant controlled but steady economic exploitation, whereas park-style preservation was virtually a "waste" of natural resources.

The election of Governor James N. Gillett in November 1906 brought many changes to state government. One relatively obscure change was the replacement of Warden Pilkington with a sixty-five-year-old Boulder Creek merchant and former state senator by the name of Samuel H. Rambo. Shortly after Rambo's appointment it was rumored that logging operations were underway in the park. Both Rambo and G. B. Lull, the state forester, denied that anything was wrong, however, and insisted that only dead or down timber was being removed.

Rumors of widespread and indiscriminate logging continued, and in February 1908 Andrew Hill and several other concerned citizens decided to make their own first-hand investigation. Once in the basin, they were appalled by what they found. Rounding a turn in the forest between Governor's Camp and Sempervirens Camp they could see on the hill above them "long piles of wood glistening in the sun through the few remaining trees." As Hill put it, there was "wood, wood, wood everywhere. Pickets and posts and split timber over acres of ground, as far as the eye could see." Nor was all this wood being cut exclusively from dead or down timber. There were, according to Hill, "many green redwood trees, the cleanest, largest and best specimens in that part of the park, alive, unburned, with green leaves upon them, cut down; some all cut into wood or posts but the stumps, others half cut, and so on."

The expedition's report, backed up by Hill photographs, soon led to a grand jury investigation and an end to further logging in the park. And shortly after his inauguration in 1911, the popular and highly respected reform governor, Hiram Johnson, saw to it that California Redwood Park was taken out of the hands of the foresters and lumbermen, and put back under the control of a park commission like the original one—selected on a non-partisan basis and made up of interested citizens and relevant academic specialists, plus the governor, ex-officio.

Hill and the Sempervirens Club had long felt that better access routes were needed so that more people would be able to enjoy the scenic and botanical wonders of Big Basin. Early efforts to improve access had been cut short by the general chaos surrounding the great earthquake and fire of April 1906. Hill himself lost all of his paintings, photographs, and photographic equipment—an economic and professional setback from which he never fully recovered. The road question was further delayed by the forestry and logging controversy of 1907-08, but finally in 1912 the time seemed right, and a major campaign was launched to gain legislative support for better access to the basin.

Before it was over this new campaign very nearly matched in magnitude the widespread public involvement that had created the park in the first place. Literally thousands of people contributed time and money to the campaign itself, and to a fund for acquiring rights-of-way for those portions of the road that would pass through private property. The counties of Santa Clara, Santa Cruz, and San Mateo paid for a survey of the route, and in 1913 with all of the legislative conditions met, the state appropriated $70,000 for actual construction work. By 1915, in time to serve visitors to the fabulous Panama-Pacific International Exhibition in San Francisco, the road was open and the park could be used—as it is today—for short one-day trips by residents of the San Francisco Bay Area, as well as by vacationers and overnight campers from throughout the state and nation.

3 The Historic Preservation Movement

"Our parks and preserves are not merely picnicking places. They are rich storehouses of memories and reveries. They are bearers of wonderful tales to him who will listen, a solace to the aged and an inspiration to the young."

Colonel Richard Lieber

Left: *Statue of James W. Marshall shortly after completion in February 1889, ready for shipment to the Marshall Monument at Coloma. A piece of gold lies in the open palm of the right hand. The index finger of the left hand will point to the spot on the American River where Marshall made his momentous discovery.* Below: *James W. Marshall, wheelwright, carpenter, discoverer of gold.*

The creation of parks at Yosemite and Big Basin as well as the creation of city and national parks elsewhere in California throughout the late nineteenth and early twentieth centuries, indicated the growing strength of what might be called the "park movement." At roughly the same time, interest in historical preservation was also growing. Today historical parks, monuments, and landmarks are such an integral part of the State Park System that it is a bit surprising to realize that these two interests were once quite separate and distinct from one another. The fact is, nevertheless, that the earliest state historic parks were created at a time when the word "park" was rarely if ever used by those who were interested in historical preservation.

Widespread public interest in California history can be traced largely to interest in the great California gold rush. That phase of the California story is so dramatic and unusual that people everywhere have been fascinated by it. Even those who actually participated in the gold rush seem to have been impressed by its historical importance, for despite all the excitement and turmoil, it was a rather self-conscious moment. History was clearly being made, and many a fortyniner or other pioneer was fully aware that he or she was participating in a saga the whole world was watching and would long remember. This historical self-awareness was expressed in many ways including place names that commemorated both immediate gold rush realities and the earlier Spanish-Mexican era that was being displaced. It was also expressed by the formation of the Society of California Pioneers in 1850 and by the incorporation of the Historical Society of California in 1852.

In 1853 perhaps the first official state expenditure on behalf of historic preservation occurred when the painter William S. Jewett received $5,000 from the California Legislature for a portrait of John Sutter, one of the state's most famous pioneers. Ironically, even as the painting went on display in the state capitol at Benicia, Sutter himself was rapidly being stripped of his vast holdings in the Sacramento Valley. Still only 50 years old, he was in effect already an historic artifact—a rather elegant, charming, and harmless reminder of an

era that had ended literally overnight with James Marshall's discovery of gold in the tail-race of Sutter's mill at Coloma.

Public interest in California history declined somewhat during the later, less exciting years of the gold rush and especially during the Civil War years. Nevertheless, a number of individuals including Hubert Howe Bancroft, a San Francisco book dealer and man of letters, continued to pay attention to California and western American history. Bancroft's far ranging historical research and publication program began in 1859 and continued very actively over the next 30 years. In 1905 his unique collection of books, papers, and related historical materials became a public archive when the University of California purchased the collection and set up the Bancroft Library as a division of its main library.

Renewed interest in historical matters was shown during the 1870s by the revival of the California Historical Society and by the creation of several new organizations including the Native Sons of the Golden West. The adventurous young men of 1849 were getting on in years, and a wistful quality surrounded them; in most cases the extravagant hopes and dreams of earlier years had fallen far short of fulfillment. Even James Marshall, the very man whose discovery of gold had set off the great California rush of 1849, had failed to prosper. By the 1870s he had fallen on hard times. Paying tribute to Marshall and his momentous role in the history of California, the legislature of 1872 voted to provide him with a pension of $200 per month. This was cut to $100 in 1874 and stopped altogether in 1878 as a result of his repeated and bad-tempered fits of public drunkenness.

Brooding and bitter, Marshall was difficult to honor during his lifetime, but soon after his death in 1885 the Native Sons of the Golden West set out to memorialize him and his discovery through the creation of the state's first official historic landmark. In 1887, the legislature agreed with the Native Sons and called for a granite monument and bronze statue of Marshall to be erected at his grave overlooking the gold discovery site at Coloma. In 1890, 25 five acres of land surrounding the mon-

Johann Augustus Sutter, pioneer, founder and commandant of New Helvetia, guardian of the Sacramento frontier.

ument were donated to the state by the Native Sons. On May 3 of that year the monument was ceremoniously dedicated and opened to the public.

Interest in California history and historic preservation continued to mount throughout the 1880s and '90s. In 1882, restoration work was begun on the old Spanish mission at Carmel, and the subsequent location and marking of the grave of Padre Junipero Serra stirred surprisingly widespread public interest. The ruins of Sutter's Fort in Sacramento were threatened with complete obliteration in 1888 by a proposal to extend a city street straight through the middle of the site. Though the fort had suffered complete neglect for many years, this threat brought strong public reaction. Giving leadership to public sentiment, the statewide organization of the Native Sons of the Golden West raised $20,000 toward acquisition and restoration of the fort. Charles F. Crocker personally subscribed $15,000 for this purpose.

In 1891, the Native Sons and others persuaded the legislature to accept title to the property and to provide another $20,000 for further restoration work. The legislature also voted to create a Sutter's Fort Board of Commissioners that would administer both the fort and the Marshall Monument at Coloma. Two years later, on April 26, 1893, the fort was officially dedicated and opened to public visitation as a state historic monument.

Rising interest in the preservation of historic sites was also evident in the southern part of the state where the Southern California Landmarks Club was formed in 1894 to rescue some of the great old California mission structures. This group was organized and led by Charles F. Lummis, the colorful, eloquent, and persuasive editor-writer-

photographer who, after the turn of the century, went on to inspire the creation of the Southwest Society and the Southwest Museum in Los Angeles. This museum group was dedicated to the collection and preservation of southwestern archeological materials, and to increased understanding and appreciation of those older, quieter ways of life that had been lived in the vast reaches of the old Southwest by Indian and Spanish-speaking peoples prior to the arrival of Anglo society.

The 1880s and '90s also saw the formation of other important historical associations including the Historical Society of Southern California (in 1884), the Native Daughters of the Golden West (in 1886), and the California Historical Society, which was reorganized and resurrected once again in 1886-87—this time with the involvement of professional historians associated with the University of California and other institutions of higher learning. An increasing number of books and periodicals dealing with California history became available during the 1880s and '90s, including Bancroft's extraordinary, multi-volumed history of California and the West.

The purpose of all this historical interest and activity varied from the genealogical to the philosophical, from the silly and superficial to the most thoughtful and scholarly evaluation of past events.

In a paper entitled "The Value of a Historical Society," published by the Historical Society of Southern California in 1899, Walter R. Bacon described the practical importance of a broad general awareness of past events:

"No country or community advances except through the patriotism of its people; it might be said, the *intelligent* patriotism of its people. Patriotism is love of country, and intelligent patriotism is only possible when the patriot knows of the lives, deeds and characters of the citizens of his country who have served it so as to make it worthy of his patriotic love. . . . Historical philosophy alone," Bacon said, "can tabulate the mistakes, point out the pitfalls to be avoided, fully appraise the advantages gained and mark a course for future pursuit which will preserve to us the best and discard the valueless."

The geographically more specific

and less abstract work of local historical associations, Bacon concluded, had a different yet equally important role to play. Such associations could spread historical awareness to the general population by finding ways to dramatize the fact that an area's pioneers "lived under the same skies that we now see," and were "shadowed" by the same mountains that still mark the horizon. The collection, preservation, and display of historical artifacts of local relevance, Bacon pointed out, could engage the interest of many who would otherwise remain unaware of historical matters, and who would therefore be unable to learn from the historical record.

Around the turn of the century the importance of local history was more widely recognized, and some people were convinced that public interest in historical matters could best be generated by systematically marking, identifying, celebrating, and preserving historic sites and buildings. Formal recognition of historic landmarks would help to keep the past alive not just for professional historians or members of historical associations, but for the whole society on a continuing basis, generation after generation. As this point of view gained popular support, it was also recognized that most of the buildings and other sites best suited to serve as landmarks were rapidly disappearing.

Responding to this crisis early in 1902, the Native Sons of the Golden West created a Landmarks Committee to "investigate and report upon the condition of the remaining historic buildings throughout the state, and to suggest practical methods for their preservation and restoration." The committee was to be chaired by a promising young man from Oakland by the name of Joseph R. Knowland, who shortly after his appointment called together some of the many organizations interested in California history, and asked them to join forces in an alliance to be known as the California Historical Landmark League. Only 29 years old, Knowland was already an established civic leader and political activist who had served two terms in the state assembly, and was soon to move on to the state senate. It should be noted, however, that although Know-

Monterey Custom House circa 1895.

land was active in partisan politics, both the Native Sons and the new Landmark League were strictly non-partisan organizations in which Democrats and Republicans worked together with a single spirit.

The stated purpose of the Landmark League was to "preserve the historic landmarks of the state—notably the old missions; to place in appropriate places memorial tablets commemorative of historic places and events; to encourage historical research; and to use all proper means to establish a chair of California history at the University of California." In order to accomplish any or all of their objectives, funds were needed.

The league's fund-raising campaign got off to a running start in September 1902 when the "Joint Committee of 1900," another arm of the Native Sons of the Golden West, turned over $1,100 to the new Landmark League. Funds accumulated even more rapidly in 1903, when William Randolph Hearst put the full resources of the *San Francisco Examiner* and the rest of his newspaper empire squarely behind the Landmark League's campaign. The results were so gratifying that Hearst was named principal trustee of all funds held by the league.

The league assured everyone that

all of its restoration projects would be reviewed by a distinguished advisory committee made up of leading artists and architects, and representatives of the state's leading educational institutions including David Starr Jordan of Stanford, Benjamin Ide Wheeler of the University of California, and the Reverend Robert E. Kenna of Santa Clara University. The goal was "artistic design" and "intelligent restoration" that would preserve the integrity of California's old mission buildings and other

California First Theater circa 1900.

historic sites. As Knowland put it, "the founders of the league believed that it was better to allow the old missions of California to crumble than to attempt modernization."

Moving on a broad front and with enthusiastic support from the California State Automobile Association and the Automobile Club of Southern California as well as other groups, the league sponsored state legislation in 1903 calling for preservation of Colton Hall in Monterey, site of the California Consti-

tutional Convention of 1847. A bronze plaque was designed and placed on "Fort Gunnybags," the headquarters in 1856 of San Francisco's controversial Committee of Vigilance. Also in 1903, a survey of the remaining Spanish mission buildings was carried out in cooperation with the Southern California Landmarks Club, which had already spent some $5,000 on mission restoration projects in southern California.

The Landmark League found that Mission San Antonio de Padua in Monterey County had fallen into a state of complete neglect. To save the old mission buildings from further distintegration, the league negotiated a ten-year lease and obtained permission to attempt at least partial restoration. By November 1903, several thousand dollars' worth of restoration work had been carried out including the provision of a temporary wooden roof that would protect the adobe walls of the building. Architectural work for the project was contributed by an officer of the league, and, as Knowland later said, once construction funds were exhausted, "a number of poor Indians and local people of Spanish descent donated a week's work toward completion of the project—an example to all Californians."

From 1903 to 1906 the league spon-

sored a series of illustrated lectures designed to generate public sentiment for further landmarks work. The league also provided funds for scholarships and historical research at the University of California. But perhaps the most visible, best known, and most enduring accomplishment of the league was the acquisition of several important historic sites and buildings: the Mission of San Francisco Solano at Sonoma, the ground surrounding the landing place of Junipero Serra at Monterey, the his-

Serra Monument. On the site of El Castillo in Monterey, overlooking the Serra Landing Place of 1770. Monument unveiled June 3, 1981, the gift of Mrs. Leland Stanford.

toric Russian settlement known as Fort Ross, and California's first theater in Monterey.

As trustees for the cash and real property held by the California Landmark League, William Randolph Hearst took title to these sites and signed them over one by one to the State of California. The league itself, however, was fading away by the time the last of these gift deeds was signed in November 1906, and thereafter California landmark preservation work was carried on by the many organizations and individuals who had temporarily joined together to form the league.

For his part, Joseph R. Knowland continued to be actively involved in California historic landmark matters throughout the next half century and more—until his death in 1966 at the age of 92. His tenure as chairman of the Landmarks Committee, N. S. G. W., spanned a full 60 years, and though he spent five and one-half terms in Congress (1904-14), took controlling interest in the Oakland Tribune in 1915, and was busy with a myriad of other concerns, Knowland always found time to pursue his interest in California landmarks and related historical preservation work. Year after year, he took time to organize and participate in special events—the annual gold discovery celebration at Coloma, for example—designed to stimulate greater public interest in the history of California and the West. Moreover, he was a member of the State Park Commission for 24 years, and chairman of that body for nearly 20 years.

Women and women's groups also played an important role in the historic landmark and historic preservation movement. The drive to preserve Pio Pico Mansion, for example, began in 1905 when the Women's Club of Whittier joined with the East Whittier Women's Club and the Women's Auxiliary of the Whittier Board of Trade to form the Pio Pico Historical and Museum Society. Pico was the last governor of the Mexican province of Alta California and a man of great personal charm. Museum Society members were convinced that Pico's memory and the remains of his rambling 34-room house provided a unique opportunity to capture and portray for later generations something of the gracious lifestyle of

Laying the cornerstone, Pioneer Monument, June 10, 1910. Principal speaker: Congressman Joseph R. Knowland, President, Grand Parlor, Native Sons of the Golden West.
Below: *Pioneer Monument dedication, June 6, 1918, with survivors of the Donner Party in attendance.*

California's pastoral pre-gold rush period.

With help from the Whittier Board of Trade the society persuaded the City of Whittier to acquire the Pico mansion and then lease it back to the society for restoration and public display. Funds were raised, preliminary restoration work was carried out, and in 1909 the mansion was opened to the public. In 1914, hoping to obtain additional funds for restoration work, the City of Whittier gift-deeded the site to the State of California.

By 1940 the Native Daughters of the Golden West (177 parlors in 50 counties) had out-organized the Native Sons (136 parlors in 44 counties) to become probably the most broadly based citizens' organization in California dedicated to historical matters — another indication of the strong interest California women have taken in the history of the state.

The many chapters—or parlors, as they were called—of the Native Sons

and Daughters of the Golden West always worked closely with other local groups on behalf of specific landmark projects. During the first decades of the 20th century, the most notable of these projects included the Monterey Custom House, the Pioneer Monument (often called the Donner Monument) near Donner Lake, San Pasqual Battlefield in San Diego County, the Bear Flag Monument in historic Sonoma Plaza, the site of the tragic 1859 duel between Broderick and Terry near San Francisco, the Marshall Blacksmith Shop Museum in Kelsey (near Placerville), and Petaluma Adobe, the great old adobe building that was the center of life on Mariano Vallejo's vast rancho near Petaluma.

Some of these landmarks required not only the generosity and financial support of private interests, but also extraordinary determination, patience, and persistence on the part of sponsoring groups. It was 1898, for instance, when agitation began for a monument that would honor the overland pioneers of the 1840s and '50s including the ill-fated Donner Party. But not until 20 years later, on June 6, 1918, was it possible for the governors of California and Nevada and a group of distinguished citizens to gather near the shore of Donner Lake just below the summit of Donner Pass and dedicate the completed monument. Moreover, it was not until June 1928 that the state accepted title to the monument and $25,000 worth of land around it—a gift to the people from the Native Sons of the Golden West.

Efforts to preserve the Custom House in Monterey stretched out over an even longer period. Landmark status for the building had been sought as early as the 1880s, but various political factors, local commercial interests, and a prolonged dispute over land titles involving both the state and federal governments, effectively blocked ownership and administration of the building as an historical landmark. The Native Sons of the Golden West, however, did manage to lease the building from the U.S. Treasury Department for $1.00 per year starting in 1900. In 1903 they persuaded the State of California to take over the lease and provide funds for restoration. The state appointed a Monterey Custom House Board of Trustees to

look after the building, and in 1917 provided additional restoration funds. But not until 1929, on the eighty-third anniversary of the American capture of Monterey, was the old Custom House opened to the public as a state historic monument. And not until 1938, with matching funds provided by local citizens, did the State Park System manage to acquire the building.

State legislation in 1915 created a California Historical Survey Commission, which was to be headquartered at the University of California in Berkeley and charged with the responsibility of evaluating and coordinating historic preservation proposals on a statewide basis. Annual appropriations for this purpose were provided by the legislature until 1923 when the Survey Commission was replaced by the California State Historical Association, an ambitious but loosely organized affiliation of historical groups from all parts of the state. This new association received some funding from the state, and survived until World War II, but was never able to generate the widespread public support it had hoped for. It did manage to improve communication among the growing number of groups interested in California history, but under the trusteeship of the State Board of Education it emphasized research and publication, and did not develop further administrative interest in state historic landmarks.

Actual administration of the monuments remained in the hands of various relatively independent boards and commissions, several of which theoretically included the governor or were supposed to report directly to him. This arrangement was changed somewhat in 1921 by a reorganization of state government that placed the monuments and their volunteer administrative boards and commissions under the jurisdiction of the Department of Finance. This was a slightly more realistic administrative arrangement, but the state still had no mechanism whereby it could direct and administer a balanced statewide program of historic preservation. That would have to await the creation of a single, overall commission charged with the responsibility of creating and coordinating a statewide system of both parks and historic monuments.

4 Save the Redwoods!

> **"The state of civilization of a people may be measured by its care and forethought for the welfare of generations to come."**
>
> *Dr. John C. Merriam*
> *Founders Grove Dedication*
> *September 13, 1931*

Newton B. Drury

The opening years of the twentieth century had seen the creation of California Redwood Park in Big Basin and rising interest in the preservation of other small southerly portions of California's coastal redwood forest. For a time, however, the magnificent primeval redwoods of the north coast region remained little known to the public and too remote for extensive logging operations.

Naturalists had explored the forests of the north coast region, and some, including John Muir, were especially impressed by the extraordinary stand of redwoods alongside the South Fork of the Eel River at Bull Creek and the nearby Dyerville Flat. These experts agreed that the coast redwood forest was at its magnificent best far to the north of San Francisco. Some authorities went so far as to say that the Bull Creek and Dyerville Flat area supported the most impressive and spectacular forest in the whole world. Here the redwoods were unusually and almost uniformly large and tall and symmetrical. They formed a pure stand of old redwoods—a stand so dense that other kinds of trees could not survive in the deep shade of the canopy formed by 300-foot-high redwoods.

Knowledgeable lumbermen also looked upon the Bull Creek area with great respect and agreed among themselves that it probably held more timber, more potential board feet of lumber per acre, than any forest they had ever seen. The area was owned by the Pacific Lumber Company, but was considered too inaccessible for commercial logging operations.

In 1916 and 1917 several developments took place that would eventually have a profound impact on the north coast redwood region in general and the Bull Creek-Dyerville Flat area in particular. First of all, the National Park Service was created in 1916, and under the inspired leadership of its first director, Stephen T. Mather, set out to acquire for public "use, resort, and recreation" those features of North America that could best remind Americans of their pioneer tradition, and of the magnificent natural heritage that everyone had a right to enjoy and a responsibility to preserve. According to Mather and other park advocates, the unique and highly scenic redwood forest that grew along the western edge of the continent was one feature of the American landscape that clearly merited national recognition and preservation through park status. From the national point of view, the north coast redwoods were not inaccessible. They were, in fact, easier to visit than other national treasures, such as Yellowstone, that had already become national parks.

The second major factor affecting Bull Creek and the north coast redwoods was the construction of a new state highway through the redwoods to Eureka and Crescent City in the extreme northwest corner of California. This new highway passed right through the Bull Creek-Dyerville Flat area and promised to open up the whole South Fork of the Eel to increased tourism *and* to commercial logging. This situation was alarming to Mather and his close friend Congressman William Kent (the donor of Muir Woods and principal author of the National Park Service organic act), because virtually all of the public land in the redwood region had long since been deeded to private parties. Much of this land was now in the hands of various lumber companies.

In August 1917, a number of prominent business and professional men, academicians, and others gathered for the annual summer encampment of San Francisco's prestigious Bohemian Club. The meeting was held beneath the redwoods of the Bohemian Grove close beside the Russian River in northern California, and it was only natural in such a setting that the north coast redwood preservation issue should come up for discussion. Several members of the club were eager to have a look at the situation and before long an expedition was in the making. Mather himself was ill and unable to attend that year's encampment. In his place he had sent Horace Albright, acting director of the National Park Service. Albright himself was eager for a look at the north coast situation, but other commitments prevented him from joining the three distinguished men who finally set out on the long drive northward.

The expedition was so revealing—so impressive and yet so worrisome—that a letter was immediately written (August 9, 1917) to the governor of California, William D. Stephens, asking him

Building the highway
through Humboldt County,
1918-1919.

to find some way of preserving part of the great natural spectacle they had just witnessed.

"The forests of redwood traversed by the State Highway along the South Fork of the Eel River culminating in the superb woods of Bull Creek flats are incomparably grand... [and] should be preserved for the benefit of the people of the state through reservation as a State Park."

The letter went on to describe the creation, importance, and popular success of several prominent parks including Palisades Interstate Park in New York, which had been created by the donation of five million dollars of private funds matched by public funds from the State of New York. The letter was signed by Henry Fairfield Osborn, president of the American Museum of Natural History, New York, and was co-signed by Madison Grant, chairman of the New York Zoological Society. The third but unsigned party to this letter was Dr. John C. Merriam, professor of paleontology and Dean of the Faculties at the University of California in Berkeley.

All three of these men were scientists well known for their interest in and publications about the evolution of life on earth. All three had known John Muir and were active conservationists. Osborn and Muir, particularly, had been close personal friends and had worked together, along with Robert Underwood Johnson, to save Yosemite National Park from devastation by the Hetch Hetchy water project. Osborn and Grant were also close friends of Theodore Roosevelt. Grant had helped Roosevelt create the Boone and Crockett Club and other conservation-oriented groups whose general purpose was to perpetuate the American pioneering instinct and spirit of independence by preserving for public resort and recreation some significant remnants of the great American wilderness and its associated forms of wildlife. All three of these men had known one another personally and professionally for years. Now they promised to work together for the preservation of some portion of America's finest and obviously threatened primeval forest of coast redwoods.

After Osborn and Grant returned to their homes in the east, it seemed only reasonable for Merriam to assume pri-

mary responsibility for pursuing state action toward the creation of a redwood park in the north coast region. But as the months went by it became apparent that Governor Stephens and his top appointees were sympathetic but unready to act.

Redwood park prospects took an apparent turn for the worse in 1918 when Merriam decided to leave his position with the university in order to serve as president of the Carnegie Institution of Washington, D.C. Concerned that Merriam's departure from California might bring a complete halt to the redwood preservation effort, Madison Grant hurried west in August to see if he could revitalize the effort and create an organization that would be able to carry on even though Merriam, Osborn, and he himself would all be residing in the East.

Working with Highway Commissioner Charles F. Stern, Grant drafted legislation that would permit the state to acquire enough land and timber alongside highway rights of way to ensure the preservation of scenic values in the redwood region. The proposal was never officially introduced into the legislature, however, and a few months later Stern left the commission.

Grant worked with Merriam and others to form an organization that he said should be called the "Save-the-Redwoods League." A charter was drawn up along with a statement of purpose and a list of prospective vice-presidents and other officers. A membership drive was designed that would start with faculty members of the colleges and universities of California and the West. If a positive response could be obtained, the drive would be broadened to include residents of the redwood region as well as business and industrial leaders in California and elsewhere across the nation.

In Washington, D.C., in October 1918, Grant and Merriam met with Franklin K. Lane, then Secretary of the Interior and clearly, as was said at the time, a "Californian of national standing." They discussed the redwood situation in California and with Mather's help persuaded Lane to serve as president of the new league.

In June 1919, the league discovered that the postwar building boom was affecting the lumber market. Logging

operators, trying hard to keep up with demand, were taking the trees that were easiest to reach. As a result, big redwoods right alongside the state highway in Humboldt County were being cut. One eyewitness described the scene as worse than a World War I battlefield. Clearly the time had come for the league to take effective action.

In Washington, Mather succeeded in having a resolution passed by Congress calling for a survey of national redwood park possibilities. The resolution also directed the Secretary of the Interior to determine "whether or not the whole or any part of such lands or the purchase price thereof would be donated to the United States." This was as much as could be expected from Congress at the time, for as Mather, Albright, and other leading park advocates in Washington were fully aware, Congress had consistently refused to acquire private land for park purposes. All of the national parks up to that time had been carved out of the public domain or donated to the nation by public agencies or private individuals.

In August, Mather and Madison Grant came west in time to attend the first meeting of the board of directors of the Save-the-Redwoods League. Held in the Palace Hotel in San Francisco, this was the meeting at which the league's officers and its statement of purpose were officially adopted. Shortly afterward Mather and Grant proceeded northward to take a first-hand look at the redwood logging situation in Humboldt County, to stir up local enthusiasm for redwood preservation efforts, and to publicize the need for an intelligent, long-range program of preservation.

In several places close beside the highway as they traveled northward, they saw gigantic and truly ancient redwoods being cut down and used not to manufacture finished lumber, but simply to make "split" products such as grape stakes and railroad ties. As Grant later put it, this was rather like "breaking up one's grandfather clock for kindling to save the trouble of splitting logs at the woodpile."

Mather and Grant vowed to do what they could to stop this unnecessary destruction of redwoods, and they found the citizens of Humboldt County eager to help. A special delegation led by A.

Bull Creek Flat, 1919.

E. Connick, president of the First National Bank of Eureka, came south to meet Mather and Grant near Bull Creek and escort them to Eureka where the Chamber of Commerce staged a big rally and reception in their honor. The next day more meetings were held including a luncheon attended by the governor of California, William Stephens.

At these meetings resolutions were adopted that asked the logging operators to refrain—voluntarily—from cutting those redwoods that were within or near the highway right-of-way.

The larger operators immediately agreed to this request, but it soon became clear that the kind of delay that was being requested would mean financial disaster for the small operators. To solve this problem Mather pledged $15,000 of his own money, and another $15,000 from William Kent. The money could be used, Mather said, to acquire redwoods alongside the highway, provided only that Humboldt County put up an equal amount for the same purpose. It was the kind of gesture—big, generous, inspiring, patriotic—that had already made Mather into something of a folk hero, a legend in his own time.

In the ensuing euphoria several other private gifts of land and timber were offered to the county by local owners. On August 9, 1919, Mather was able to say with some confidence that the north coast redwoods would be saved. Shortly afterward, Humboldt County voted to match the Kent-Mather gift and acquire as many highway-related redwood areas as it could afford. The campaign to save the redwoods was underway.

Since the federal government could not be counted on to save a representative example of the nation's redwoods through the creation of a national redwood park, it was obvious that the redwoods could only be saved through the activity of private individuals working in cooperation with state and county governments. In any case, it was going to be necessary to build a broad base of public support. In order to do this— to solicit members, raise funds, and work with county governments and the state legislature—the league decided to hire a promising young executive whose public relations and advertising firm, the Drury Company, was making

a name for itself representing commercial clients and a number of educational institutions such as the University of California.

Newton B. Drury was then thirty years old. The son of Wells Drury, a popular western newspaper editor, Newton had grown up with a strong interest in music and literature as well as public affairs. A part-time newspaper reporter, and a music and drama critic while still in high school, Drury specialized in literature and rhetoric as a student at the University of California where he was also a highly regarded member of the debate team and president of the student body during his senior year. After graduation in 1912 he served as an administrative assistant to university president Benjamin Ide Wheeler, and was an instructor in English literature and forensics. Thus it was a broad academic background, a wide range of acquaintances, and extraordinary diplomatic and persuasive skill that Drury brought to his work on behalf of the league.

The league began to prosper immediately. Through Mather's influence with eastern editors and Drury's practical support on the west coast, articles about the league and its objectives appeared in national magazines including the *Saturday Evening Post, National Geographic,* and *Natural History Magazine.* Osborn's article in *Natural History* explained that redwood parks would have to be acquired first of all by private funds donated to the league. Redwood forest lands thus acquired would then be presented "to Uncle Sam" and would constitute "definite recognition of the unitedness of government and people in America."

Membership in the league increased steadily and enthusiasm for its objectives was widespread, but funds for acquisition of redwood forest land did not accumulate in the league treasury as rapidly as had been hoped. This became a critical problem in late 1920 when A. E. Connick reported from Eureka that roadside logging operations could not be postponed much longer. The small operators had been bought out by the county according to the terms of the 1919 agreement with Kent and Mather. But the larger operators were still holding back on a strictly voluntary basis—with Connick struggling

to assure them that the league would come up with some money to buy them out.

In order to meet this crisis, the league worked out a precise statement of goals and a definite strategy for achieving them. Four redwood areas would be sought, each an example of a different ecological situation within the redwood region. Total acreage to be acquired would depend on the amount of funding that could be obtained, but the league's long-range objective was uncompromisingly idealistic even in its least ambitious form. Funds were also to be raised and provided for scientific study of the coast redwood, and for educational programs that would increase public understanding and appreciation of the redwood story, past and present.

To achieve its redwood preservation goals the league agreed to strive for the creation—the *eventual* creation— of a large national park. More immediately, however, the league would concentrate on raising private funds and on legislative proposals leading to the creation of state redwood parks. As an additional incentive to private philanthropy, the league set up a program whereby individuals, groups, and even ideas could be honored in an impressive and lasting way through the acquisition and preservation of suitably named and dedicated "memorial groves."

Many people helped carry on the program of the league, but the spirit behind the movement was that of Dr. John C. Merriam. Although his work as president of the Carnegie Institution kept him in Washington most of the time, he stayed in close touch with the day-to-day activity of the league by telegram, telephone, and a steady flow of correspondence with Newton Drury. Moreover, each summer, starting in 1919, Merriam managed to spend some time in the West continuing the academic work that had made him an authority on plant and animal evolution. On each of these trips he also took time to review the league's program and deliver an annual message to the council of the league.

These annual messages—particularly those after 1921 when he replaced Franklin K. Lane as president of the league—set the tone and direction of

Dedication of the Franklin K. Lane Grove, Sunday, August 24, 1924. John C. Merriam speaking. Newton Drury to his right.

league activity throughout the next two decades. To this day these annual messages remain interesting and inspirational, for Merriam brought to them a rare mixture of scientific information and philosophical and aesthetic concerns. With all the power, prestige, and credibility of the scientific and academic communities behind him, he maintained that certain areas should be preserved in their wilderness condition, not to withhold them from use, but precisely so that they might be used for their best and highest purposes—as natural temples, as places where the human mind and spirit might be free to explore and observe, and thereby be renewed, strengthened, recreated.

In 1921 the league pursued legislation that promised to provide $300,000 of state money to supplement the funds already being expended by the league and by Humboldt County for acquisition of redwood forest land adjacent to the state highway in southern Humboldt County. Carefully written and amended to make it acceptable to the various lumber interests in Humboldt County, the bill was unopposed and eventually passed the legislature by an almost unanimous vote. Despite this indication of general approval, Governor Stephens was reluctant to sign the bill because the state was faced with a $14 million deficit that year. On behalf of the Save-the-Redwoods League, Drury made sure that the governor heard from interested groups and individuals all around the state, including the California Federation of Women's Clubs in which the governor's wife was very active. In April, a delegation of league members called upon the governor in person.

Governor Stephens was very polite and friendly. The arguments offered on behalf of the redwood acquisition legislation were earnest, and Drury, in particular, was eloquent. Albright of the National Park Service assured the governor that, at least in his personal opinion, "state action on this matter would pave the way for a federal appropriation... [and would constitute] the first step toward the ultimate establishment of a national redwood park further north." But the governor remained unsure of his course.

The state was short of funds, he said,

and there were many other problems, many uncertainties. There might not even be enough money to keep the schools open. The governor was especially worried about the schools. Finally, William Kent, who had known Stephens for many years and served with him in Congress, could stand it no longer. Bursting out of his chair and crossing the room he slammed his fist down on the governor's desk.

"Hell, Bill!" he said to the governor. "Close the schools! The kids will love it and they can make up the work. But this can't wait. If those trees are cut it'll take a thousand years to grow new ones!"

The governor smiled at his old friend but still refused to commit himself. In June, however, he approved the legislation and thereafter Solon Williams of the Forestry Board was able to acquire several redwood groves alongside the highway adjacent to the South Fork of the Eel River in what is now Humboldt Redwoods State Park. One of these areas, Richardson Grove, included a campground, rental cabins, and other tourist accommodations that were suitable for public use and management by concession contract.

On August 6, 1921, the league staged its first memorial grove dedication. Purchased by the league with funds from Dr. John C. Phillips of Wenham, Massachusetts, the grove was intended to honor the memory of Phillips' brother-in-law Colonel Reynaud C. Bolling, the first American officer of high rank to be killed in action in World War I. As one of the principal speakers that day, Madison Grant stressed the patriotic implications of redwood preservation in an address entitled "Preserve an America Worth Fighting For." The event was widely publicized and apparently struck a responsive chord in the American spirit, for the memorial grove program steadily increased in popularity until, by 1928, it was providing approximately one-third of the league's total income.

As the Save-the-Redwoods League preservation program became increasingly successful during the early 1920s, the owners of forest land in the north coast region became restless. They wanted to know just which areas the league wished to acquire and preserve, and which areas the lumber companies

could harvest or at least plan to harvest. A comprehensive survey of the redwood region was needed in order for the league and the state to draw up a long-range plan for state parks in the redwood region.

Several legislative proposals were submitted in 1923 that called for the acquisition of redwood areas on one basis or another. All of these bills died in the legislature except one, AB 106, which had the backing of William Randolph Hearst and other influential citizens, as well as the support of several north coast lumber companies. Submitted by Assemblyman Albert Rosenshine of San Francisco, AB 106 enabled the State Board of Forestry to accept and administer any redwood park areas that might be given to the state by private parties or local governmental agencies. The bill also called for a survey of potential park sites in the redwood region.

The league was not enthusiastic about the Rosenshine bill because it meant that state park acquisition decisions might be made by anyone who chose to acquire land and give it to the state for park purposes. The league wanted park acquisition decisions to be made by an official state agency on the basis of the best available professional advice. The league and lumber interests agreed on the need for an official, state-sponsored, comprehensive survey of potential redwood parks. But even though AB 106 was approved by the legislature and signed by the governor, no funds were provided for survey work. The only survey work that got done in 1923-24, therefore, was that paid for by the league itself. This partial and preliminary survey work was still underway in November 1924 when, to the dismay of league members, the Pacific Lumber Company started cutting trees at Dyerville Flat.

Negotiations between the league and the Pacific Lumber Company concerning the incomparable forest at Dyerville Flat and Bull Creek had been underway for several years. The area was central to the interests of both the league and Pacific Lumber, but Pacific Lumber owned the area and was simply unwilling to sell it—unwilling even to put a price on it. The only way the league could hope to save it from being logged off was through govern-

Dedication of the Bolling Grove, August 6, 1921. Front row, left to right: *J. C. Sperry, William H. Crocker, Madison Grant, E. C. Bradley, Dr. John C. Merriam.* Second row: *Donald McDonald, between Sperry and Crocker.*

mental intervention, and that was seemingly impossible because no governmental agency had both the willingness and the funds to acquire the area.

Even if the league could supply the funds, the congressional track record on matters of this kind made it clear that the federal government would not intervene. The State of California was very unlikely to step in because California forestry matters were in the hands of the State Board of Forestry— a body that had repeatedly shown itself to be subservient to the interests of the lumber industry. The Forestry Board, in fact, had known about the Pacific Lumber Company's logging operations for a full week without ever notifying Humboldt County, the Save-the-Redwoods League, or any other preservation-minded group.

With both state and federal action fairly well out of the question, it was clear that intervention by Humboldt County was the only real hope of preserving the Dyerville Flat and Bull Creek redwoods. It was also clear that Humboldt County did not have funds enough to proceed with acquisition. The league would have to solve that problem.

Immediately after learning of the emergency, Drury alerted key members of the league by telephone and telegram. A second set of telegrams also went out asking Pacific Lumber to stop cutting and resume negotiations. They refused.

On the east coast, John Merriam got in touch with Madison Grant, who had been pursuing a very promising line of discussion with John D. Rockefeller, Jr. regarding a large donation to the league. Now, in a flurry of action, more information was requested by Rockefeller and his advisors, and it was immediately supplied by the league through Merriam and Grant. On November 24, 1924, just five days after the league had first heard about the logging operation at Dyerville, Grant was able to wire William Crocker, a member of the league and president of Crocker National Bank in San Francisco, advising him to proceed with negotiations for "as large an area in both the Bull Creek and Dyerville tracts as is obtainable." In this endeavor the league could count on up to one million dollars, but under no circumstances was anyone to say anything about who

had provided the money. The Rockefellers had learned through bitter experience that even the slightest mention of their name could set off a wave of speculation.

After trying and failing once again to reach a satisfactory agreement with the Pacific Lumber Company, the league offered to provide acquisition funds to Humboldt County if the county would agree to acquire the Dyerville Flat-Bull Creek redwoods by condemnation, if necessary. In Eureka, on November 26, after a very stormy and dramatic public hearing, the Humboldt County Board of Supervisors agreed to proceed with acquisition of both Dyerville Flat and Bull Creek Flat. The County also obtained a court order that immediately prohibited further logging.

The short-term emergency was over, but the long and difficult process of public acquisition was just beginning. Years would go by before a settlement could be reached. But early in the negotiations one conclusion began to seem inevitable to the men of the league: in order to negotiate successfully with the Pacific Lumber Company and avoid destruction of the very finest coast redwoods, a larger area of the Bull Creek watershed would have to be acquired than the league had ever before dared to consider. This meant that the funds needed for acquisition were going to be far greater than anticipated. Instead of one million dollars the league might have to think in terms of four or five million—perhaps even more. This was a staggering amount of money to think of obtaining exclusively from private donations.

Faced with this dilemma the league began to give serious consideration to the possibility of a public bond act that would enable the state to acquire redwood parks using state funds matched by league and other private donations. For advice on this approach to the problem the league turned to its committee on state parks, which Merriam as league president had appointed in 1923. This committee, consisting of Duncan McDuffie, William E. Colby, and

J. C. Sperry, had been asked to outline and recommend to the league "a definite plan for a state park system and administration in California."

With Drury's help the committee had already surveyed state park programs around the nation. Valuable assistance in this endeavor was provided by the National Conference on State Parks, an organization created by Stephen T. Mather in 1921 specifically to foster the development of state park systems. The committee also conferred with members of the Calaveras Grove Association, the Point Lobos Association, and others regarding various state park hopes and dreams.

As a result of all this research, committee chairman Duncan McDuffie advised the league that further state involvement in redwood forest preservation was most likely to come about as one element in a comprehensive, statewide park program. A whole system of parks should be created, McDuffie said, along with a single state park commission that could coordinate state park matters on a statewide basis. The still incomplete survey of park possibilities in the redwood region should cover not only the redwood belt but the entire state, and consider all possible types of state parks. To be effective, McDuffie concluded, such a survey should be made by an acknowledged expert whose word would command respect. According to McDuffie the best possible person for the job was Frederick Law Olmsted, Jr.—the son of Frederick Law Olmsted of Central Park and Yosemite fame, and a distinguished landscape architect in his own right.

Legislation would be required to create and fund the state park commission and provide funds for the survey. A bond act for state park purposes would require not only enabling legislation, but also an amendment to the state constitution that would have to be approved by a vote of the people. With Drury's help, and with advice from several key people in state government, the league's state park committee had already prepared draft legislation.

5 A Whole System of Parks

"California is growing in population more rapidly than any other state.... Unless a comprehensive plan for the preservation of recreational and scenic areas is set in motion, our children and our children's children will want for the opportunities for out of door life that make for sound bodies, clear brains and good citizenship."

Duncan McDuffie,
January 1925

Left: *Santa Monica Beach, 1928.*
Below: *Duncan McDuffie.*

At 3:30 in the afternoon on the first work day of the year 1925—Monday, January 5 —a group of leading businessmen, government leaders, and conservationists met in the Ferry Building on the San Francisco waterfront to discuss the need for legislation that would create a California State Park System. The meeting was called to order by J. D. Grant, a prominent California banker and chairman of the board of directors of the Save-the-Redwoods League. He introduced Duncan McDuffie, the tall, distinguished-looking, widely known realtor and civic activist who was also chairman of the committee on state parks for the Save-the-Redwoods League.

McDuffie reviewed the state parks of the day—five of them—"together with a score of historic monuments and places of historical interest." He pointed out that some of the parks were completely undeveloped and, as in the case of Mount Diablo, inaccessible as well. California State Redwood Park in Big Basin was, he said, "the only state park which can be said to have been adequately organized for use by the people of the State." As a whole, the state parks and historic monuments were inadequately funded and inadequately administered by a steadily increasing number of uncoordinated and unrelated boards, commissions, and state agencies. There was no fundamental policy or statewide plan for acquisition or administration of state parks and monuments. Thus, McDuffie concluded, simply on the basis of "efficiency, economy and sound administration," the state park properties demanded the immediate "creation of a state park commission with adequate powers and funds." And, he added, there were also "larger aspects of the problem."

With more and more people coming into the state and urban and industrial development proceeding rapidly in many areas, it was clear that open space and recreation opportunities would be shrinking even as the need for them increased. "It is not exaggerating the matter to say that unless a comprehensive plan for the preservation of recreational and scenic areas is set in motion, our children and our children's children will want for the opportunities for out-of-door life which make for

sound bodies, clear brains, and good citizenship."

On the economic side, preservation of scenic and recreational attractions was essential to the development of California's tourism industry. "Next to our fertile soil, California's greatest single asset is the opportunity it offers for outdoor life. No industry except agriculture puts as much money into circulation in California as do the hundreds of thousands of visitors who come here seeking health, recreation, pleasure, sport and out-of-door life generally. Yet gradually many of the attractions that have made the state famous are being destroyed like our redwood groves, or are passing into private ownership like the Monterey coastline. It would seem to be sound business for the state to see that its major opportunities for recreation and enjoyment of the out-of-doors are left open for the use and enjoyment of both its citizens and its visitors."

Vast sums of money were being invested in highway development, and as McDuffie pointed out, "more than 60 percent of the revenues to pay for this development come from the license fees and gasoline taxes paid by the owners of pleasure cars. . . . Yet the time is fast arriving when the highways will be fenced from end to end and the old opportunities for picnicking, camping and recreation which we have so enjoyed in the past will be gone forever."

Thus "our *every* interest," McDuffie concluded, "demands the creation of a state park commission to provide a centralized administration for its park lands, the making of a survey of our park needs and park possibilities, the establishment of a fundamental state park policy, and the gradual upbuilding of a State Park System."

McDuffie's comments and legislative proposals were received with great enthusiasm that day, and everyone present, including members of the California Development Association (the state chamber of commerce), agreed to support the proposals. A campaign organization, the California State Parks Committee, was formed with McDuffie as chairman, and plans were made to gather endorsements and other support for the proposed legislation. Shortly afterward, on behalf of the com-

Mount Diablo.

mittee, the Honorable Arthur H. Breed of Oakland, president pro-tem of the state senate, submitted two bills for legislative consideration. One of them, SB 185, provided for the creation of a central state park commission; the other, SB 608, set up a statewide survey of potential state park sites.

Newton B. Drury, secretary to the California State Park Committe (as well as to the Save-the-Redwoods League), was given primary responsibility for organizing public support for the two park bills. Drury immediately sent copies of McDuffie's speech to fifty leading newspapers around the state and then had it printed as a brochure for still wider distribution.

Before long the committee could point to a broad range of endorsements including the Save-the-Redwoods League itself, the Sierra Club, the Sempervirens Club, the Point Lobos Association, the Calaveras Grove Association, and other conservation groups throughout California. National organizations such as the National Parks Association, the National Conference on State Parks, the American Forestry Association, and the American Civic Association also endorsed the measures. Especially potent support was provided by the California State Automobile Association and the Automobile Club of Southern California, and by the Native Sons and Native Daughters of the Golden West and the California Federation of Women's Clubs. The boards and commissions that would be replaced or partially deprived of power by the new legislation—the California Redwood Park Commission, the Mount Diablo Park Commission, the Department of Finance, the State Board of Forestry—all announced their support. Even a number of nationally known conservationists including Stephen T. Mather, Theodore Roosevelt, and former Secretary of the Interior John Barton Payne, lent their names to the campaign.

Despite evidence of broad support (including numerous letters and telegrams to legislators), the state park commission bill ran into considerable opposition, first in the Senate Conservation Committee, and later in the Assembly Ways and Means Committee. This opposition was largely inspired by the Pacific Lumber Company and by

friends of the lumber industry including George C. Pardee, who argued, as he had in 1905 as governor of California, that all state-owned forest areas— including forest parks—should be administered by the State Board of Forestry. That agency now officially favored creation of a state park commission, but Pardee's opposition was nevertheless important, for he was still highly respected by many people in state government, especially when it came to forestry matters. Park enthusiasts, of course, remembered all too clearly the result of Pardee's 1905 decision to abolish the California Redwood Park Commission and put the redwood forests of Big Basin into the hands of the State Forester. Further complicating the situation, Donald McDonald of the Pacific Lumber Company pursuaded the California Development Association to withold its crucial endorsement. The result of all this maneuvering was a legislative compromise.

The commission bill, SB 185, was amended to make the commission more or less subject to the State Board of Control. Beyond that, all reference was stricken from the bill concerning commission ability to use the state's power of eminent domain for park purposes. Thus amended, and exhaustively debated, the bills were finally moved out of committee and subsequently approved by the legislature. All that remained to make them effective was the governor's signature.

On April 7, while the state park bills were still in committee, Newton Drury and Stephen T. Mather had visited Governor Friend William Richardson in Sacramento to discuss the bills. Though the meeting was pleasant enough, the governor indicated that he preferred by and large to see parks administered by cities, counties, and other local agencies rather than by state government. Both Mather and Drury were convinced that Richardson was completely unsympathetic to the state park movement, though several of the governor's closest friends and advisors still thought they could persuade him to sign the bills.

On June 5, the state park bills of 1925 died by "pocket veto"; the governor simply refused to sign them and instead issued a statement to the press

that he considered them "not properly drawn." According to the *Sacramento Union:* "The Governor further said the designation of commissioners was not satisfactory to him, that it did not seem necessary to create another commission at this time, and that the appropriation of $15,000 was unnecessary." Adding insult to injury, the governor also complained that the state park commission bill "was quietly slipped through the legislature without its objectionable features being discovered."

Supporters of the state park movement were disappointed by the veto and outraged by the reasons given for it. Outspoken as usual, William Kent

Governor Friend William Richardson.

described the governor's alleged reasons for vetoing the park bill as ". . . plain stupid and entirely void of vision. A blind porcupine could write just as good a commentary on the question."

The governor's precise reasons for vetoing the state park bills were lost amid a welter of partisan conflict among his close advisors and within the Republican party. One thing was clear, however; Richardson meant to stick by his pledge of economy in government.

Richardson was an extreme conservative. He had been elected in 1921 after promising drastic reductions in state spending. Once in office—true to his promise—he cut state appropria-

The summit of Mount Diablo, 1915.

tions of every kind, even those for educational and humanitarian agencies. "The schools," he announced, "must be put on a business basis. They must not only teach but practice thrift." After the legislative session of 1923, in order to limit state spending, he vetoed 411 out of 890 bills passed by the legislature. In 1925 he went even further. Of the 999 bills sent to him, he signed just 480; the rest—52 percent of that year's legislation, including the state park bills—he allowed to die.

Supporters of the state park movement had learned that partisan opposition, even the opposition of one important special interest such as the

Governor C. C. Young.

lumber industry, could be fatal. Virtually universal support for park system legislation was uniquely appropriate, for a properly conceived state park system might be expected to appeal to almost everyone. Endorsement by the non-partisan, or bi-partisan, California Development Association was almost essential. Therefore, on June 17, less than two weeks after the governor's veto, Donald McDonald, who had led the Pacific Lumber Company's fight against the state park measures, was appointed to serve along with Duncan McDuffie on a special California Development Association park committee.

McDuffie's role in state politics loomed suddenly larger when his close

friend and longtime business partner, Lieutenant Governor Clement Calhoun ("C. C.") Young, announced his candidacy for Governor in October 1925. In August 1926, with support from the Progressive Voters League, Young managed to wrest the Republican nomination away from Governor Richardson, and since Republicans vastly outnumbered Democrats in California in 1926, the Republican nomination in August virtually assued Young's victory in the general election of November 1926.

Suddenly, supporters of the state park movement could look forward to having a friend in the governor's chair. With this prospect, and on the basis of improved relations between the Save-the-Redwoods League and the Pacific Lumber Company, the rejected state park legislation of 1925 was dusted off and revised to make it more ambitious and idealistic.

Meeting in the Palace Hotel in San Francisco on February 7, 1927, the California State Parks Committee was revived as a campaign organization designed to support legislation that would create a State Park System. The meeting was attended by representatives of various conservation organizations and was presided over by Duncan McDuffie, who explained that the legislation being proposed in 1927 was an improved version of the bills passed by the legislature two years earlier. This new legislation had been reviewed and revised on the basis of advice from many people including Frederick Law Olmsted, Governor C. C. Young, and several top-level members of his administration, as well as a number of state legislators. Indications were that lumber interests would not oppose the bills this time and that enthusiastic support could be expected from the California Development Association, the major automobile clubs, local chambers of commerce, and newspapers in every part of the state.

The legislation itself, in the form of three bills, had already been submitted by State Senator Arthur H. Breed of Piedmont and Assemblyman B. J. Feigenbaum of San Francisco: Senate Bill 439 provided for the creation of a single state park commission that could coordinate and unify the administration of the entire park system;

Senate Bill 440 provided for a comprehensive survey of potential park sites throughout the state; Senate Bill 441 provided for submission to the voters of a $6 million bond issue that would provide funds for state park acquisition purposes. According to SB 441, each dollar of state funds would have to be matched by a dollar of funds or land from local or private sources before acquisition could proceed.

A fourth piece of legislation, Assembly Bill 1176, provided for the creation of a Department of Natural Resources that would combine and consolidate several existing divisions of state government. McDuffie indicated that AB 1176, sponsored by Governor Young, conflicted with the park commission bill in that it would make the proposed commission subservient to the director of the Department of Natural Resources. McDuffie indicated that the governor also favored a bond act provision that would require two dollars of local or private funds to match each dollar of state park bond funds. On this last point, however, McDuffie was still optimistic that Governor Young could be persuaded to accept the 50-50 matching principle.

All of this information was well received by the various members of the State Parks Committee, and agreement was quickly reached on matters of campaign strategy and procedure. An effort would be made to obtain the support and participation of conservation groups in every part of the state. Stenographic, printing, and postal expenses would be shared by all of the organizations involved in the campaign, but the Save-the-Redwoods League would provide the campaign headquarters, general office facilities, and the services of Newton Drury to coordinate the legislative campaign—all at no cost to the State Parks Committee.

The campaign moved smoothly and with extraordinary speed after the committee's inaugural meeting. Endorsements of the legislation flowed in from all directions. In southern California the campaign was helped along in dramatic fashion by Stephen T. Mather who made one of his typical whirlwind speaking tours. Advocates of park status for Mount San Jacinto, Santa Cruz Island, and various southern California beach areas were especially

Fort Ross circa 1928.

enthusiastic. In a quiet but important way Frederick Law Olmsted, Jr., who was then living part time in Palos Verdes, was also a factor in generating support in southern California. Soon it appeared that everyone was in favor of the legislation and no one opposed it. The time had apparently come for the state to act.

J. W. Gregg, secretary of the Pacific Coast Chapter of the American Society of Landscape Architects, probably expressed the feelings of many when he wrote to Senator Ralph E. Swing in February 1927: "The State of California is far behind many other progressive states of the Union in its adoption of a definite and systematic program for the acquirement and administration of state parks, and unless the people of this state insist that something be done along these lines immediately, the history of state parks in California will soon become a history of lost opportunities."

The state park bills of 1927 sailed through the legislative committee process without difficulty and were approved by unanimous vote in both houses. Drury, McDuffie, and other leaders of the park movement were even successful in persuading the governor and the legislature not to insist that two dollars of outside money be required to match each dollar of state money. The legislation that reached the governor's desk and that he signed on May 25, 1927, called simply for 50-50 matching as originally proposed by the State Parks Committee.

By an ironic twist of fate, the park movement enjoyed still another legislative victory in 1927—one that was completely unexpected. The state park commission bill, SB 439, was *not* superceded by AB 1176. As a result, the State Park Commission was not made subservient to the director of Natural Recources but retained full executive power over park matters. This state of affairs was the unintended result of "efficiency" on the part of Alexander R. Heron, Governor Young's director of finance. Heron, it seems, had been charged with carrying out the details of Governor Young's governmental reorganization plan. And since AB 1176 was an important part of that plan, the hard-working, wonderfully efficient Heron picked up AB 1176 as soon as it was approved by the legislature and personally rushed it to the governor for his immediate signature and a public announcement. Forgotten in the excitement over reorganization, SB 439 followed a more routine course to the governor's desk and was signed several days later.

According to normal procedure at that time, all legislation carried standard language, "boilerplate," providing for the automatic repeal of earlier, conflicting legislation. Thus, contrary to all expectations, SB 439 actually repealed portions of AB 1176—and the State Park Commission retained full executive and administrative power over the state park program. This was important to supporters of the state park movement because it meant that some extremely well-qualified people would be willing

to serve on the commission. And a commission made up of widely known and highly respected people would go a long way toward building public confidence in the state park program prior to the general election in November 1928, when the people of California would be asked to vote on the $6 million state park bond act. If funds from the bond act were not made available for acquisition of new parks, the state would still not have a park program worthy of the name.

The System Is Born

During the summer of 1927, immediately after the legislative session of that year, McDuffie, Drury, and others involved in the California State Parks Committee began to make specific arrangements for the bond campaign of 1928. McDuffie concentrated on finding the five most appropriate, most highly qualified people in California for the governor to appoint to the park commission. He excluded himself as a matter of principle, based on his close personal and business ties to the governor. Drury and McDuffie also conferred at length with Frederick Law Olmsted on a strategy for a state park survey that would produce the best possible result despite the fact that the $25,000 appropriation passed by the legislature had been reduced by the governor to $15,000. The difficulty was to design a statewide survey procedure, necessarily using a large corps of volunteers, while maintaining a high level of professional judgment about the

The first State Park Commission, left to right: *William E. Colby, Ray Lyman Wilbur, Henry W. O'Melveny, Frederick Russell Burnham, Senator Wilbur F. Chandler.*

Borrego Palm Canyon and the Laguna Mountains from Borrego Valley.

statewide significance of proposed park sites, and the relative feasibility of acquiring any one site as opposed to another.

A considerable amount of work was accomplished on all these matters by the time the state park legislation of 1927 became effective—ninety days after being signed by the governor.

In early autumn, Drury and McDuffie conferred with Governor Young about state park matters generally, and Mc-Duffie made his carefully considered recommendations concerning commission appointments. The governor, who once referred to McDuffie as his "boss when it comes to parks," immediately accepted McDuffie's recommendations.

The First State Park Commission

When the governor announced his appointments to the first genuinely statewide State Park Commision in November 1927, he also took time to describe the significance of the state park movement for people throughout the state and the nation. He mentioned the forthcoming state park survey, and pointed out that the proposed $6 million bond issue would make it possible for California "to invest for future generations $12 million in a wisely coordinated, comprehensive State Park System.

"The importance of this effort naturally demanded from me the best I could do in the selection of a Park Commission. It demanded that the Commission should be strictly non-political, and should be composed of nature lovers as well as men of pre-eminent ability and business capacity. Finally, it demanded that they should be so well and favorably known that in their efforts they will inspire the entire confidence of all our citizens."

The governor then went on to name the five men he was appointing:

William E. Colby of San Francisco was an expert in mining law and a nationally and internationally known conservationist, closely associated for many years with John Muir and numerous conservation causes and organizations, including the Sierra Club, the Save-the-Redwoods League, the American Forestry Association, the National Parks Association.

Dr. Ray Lyman Wilbur was president of Stanford University at Palo Alto, one of the original counselors of the Save-the-Redwoods League when it was founded in 1918, and an active participant in park and conservation matters in California and the nation. Wilbur went on to serve as Secretary of the Interior during the Hoover administration.

Henry W. O'Melveny of Los Angeles was a leading attorney in southern California, actively involved in civic and park matters in the southern part of the state, and a member of the Los Angeles City Park Commission since 1910.

Major Frederick Russell Burnham of Hollywood was an internationally known explorer, adventurer, and amateur archeologist, as well as the author of a then-popular book, *Scouting on Two Continents*. Burnham was a very active outdoorsman, especially well acquainted with the desert and mountain regions of southern California.

Senator Wilbur F. Chandler of Fresno was a leading San Joaquin Valley agriculturalist who had served in the state legislature from 1900 to 1916 and was active in archeological as well as in park and recreation matters.

The first meeting of the State Park Commission was a great success. Prospects were bright and morale was high. O'Melveny was later described by his lawfirm partner as "brimming over with enthusiasm for the work of the Commission and saying that he wished he had a million dollars which he could devote to the work."

At the meeting itself, held in Sacramento on December 13, 1927, various organizational and procedural matters — as well as introductions — were the principal matters of business. W. B. Rider, who had been handling state park matters for the Division of Forestry, was appointed acting chief of the newly created Division of Parks. William E. Colby was elected chairman of the commission, and both he and O'Melveny were authorized to confer with Frederick Law Olmsted and persuade him to undertake the state park

survey. The commission agreed to meet once each month, with its next meeting in Los Angeles and subsequent meetings in various cities all around the state. This policy, it was felt, would increase public awareness of the state park program as a whole, and would especially benefit the survey, in which public participation would be essential.

Meeting in Los Angeles on January 23, 1928, the State Park Commission announced the appointment of Colonel Charles B. Wing as Chief of the Division of Parks. It was a brilliant appointment. Wing was a professor of civil engineering at Stanford University and one of the most highly respected civil engineers in the West. He was also known as the very dedicated executive officer and longtime commissioner of California Redwood Park in Big Basin. He was, therefore, widely respected not only as an engineer and as an administrator, but also as a man with proven concern and sensitivity to park matters. He was, moreover, experienced in the ways of the state legislature and of state government in general.

At the Los Angeles meeting the commission also approved Olmsted's proposal for carrying out the state park survey. After some discussion they instructed Colby and Wing to have a suitable contract drawn up for official signature as soon as possible. Olmsted himself was in the East at the time of the commission meeting, but as soon as he learned of the commission's decision he cabled a member of his firm in California and advised him to get the survey underway immediately. As it turned out, the officially signed contract did not reach Olmsted until early in April. By that time a great deal had already been accomplished.

The State Park Survey

To carry out the monumental task of searching the entire state for the best possible state park sites, and in order to do this on a limited budget and

Nationally Famous Landscapist on Job Making State Parks Survey

within a limited amount of time, Olmsted invited public participation in the survey. Circulars went out to several thousand people asking for their help and advice. Olmsted also asked the commission to appoint representative citizens from all parts of the state to act as unpaid volunteer investigators and reporters. Nearly 200 people subsequently agreed to help in this way and some of them contributed very valuable advice at considerable personal cost in terms of time and travel expense.

To coordinate the flood of information that began to come in to the commission and to the survey office, and in order to investigate the more promising sites in detail, a small professional staff, including three landscape architects, was hired on a temporary basis. Regular members of the Olmsted firm also helped out with the survey. For administrative and organizational purposes, the state was divided into 12 districts following county lines and including two or more counties in each district. Reports were then compiled on the specific sites that were brought to the attention of the commission.

Along with this review of individual site proposals, Olmsted also tried to define the general policies that should guide long-range development of the system. Scenic, historic, and natural resources had to be considered in relation to population and developmental trends in order to determine which resources were most important from the park point of view, which were most critically threatened with destruction, and which could most effectively provide the public with opportunities "for enjoyment of scenery and the pleasures of nonurban outdoor life."

The survey and its purposes were widely publicized by a wonderfully cooperative press, through public hearings held by the State Park Commission, and through the activity of many civic organizations. This publicity generated a broad base of public support

and awareness as well as a flood of information. In order to further extend this base, and to help sift and analyze the available information, expert advice was sought from many individuals and organizations. The U.S. Forest Service, the National Park Service, several divisions of the State Department of Natural Resources, and the California Division of Highways were especially helpful in this regard.

College and university faculty members also provided valuable advice. Anthropology professor Alfred L. Kroeber advised Olmsted on archeological matters. Responding to a commission request, Kroeber and Olmsted discussed the possibility of restoring one or more complete Indian villages as had been done by the National Park Service in Arizona and New Mexico. Kroeber was dubious about the feasibility of such a project in California, but thought the best prospect for restoration as an "old center of religion, dance, and story" might be the Karok village of Katimin, or "some other site along the Klamath River." The old native life of California was thoroughly disrupted everywhere, he said, but on the Klamath "there are so many Indians left, and the old life was superseded so lately, that I believe a pretty effective restoration might be possible." Kroeber was enthusiastic about such a project because he felt that it "would encourage the Indians in their now rather sporadic and half-hearted efforts to revive and maintain their old dances."

Expert advice on other historical preservation projects was generously provided by university professor Charles L. Camp, and by Carl Wheat, as well as by Joseph R. Knowland and Aubrey Drury (Newton Drury's brother and associate in the Drury Company), and by organizations such as the Native Sons of the Golden West, the California Historical Society, and the Society of California Pioneers.

The State Park Bond Campaign

While the survey and the commission were reaching out to thousands of people throughout California, the state park bond campaign was reaching out to tens of thousands, even millions. The campaign got underway in early 1928 when the California State Parks

Committee was formally revived and reorganized. McDuffie was named chairman once again, and the name of the organization was changed to State Parks Council in order to minimize confusion between the campaign organization and the recently appointed State Park Commission.

Leadership for the effort again came from McDuffie, Colby, Sperry, and other members of the Save-the-Redwoods League, and the Drury Company was again hired to handle publicity and coordinate the campaign on a day-to-day basis. Funds were provided by the league itself ($2,000) and by three individuals closely associated with the league—Duncan McDuffie, J. D. Grant, and William Crocker—each of whom contributed $1,000 in January 1928. This immediate financial support got the campaign off to a running start.

In order to get things moving in southern California, Stephen T. Mather made one of his patented whirlwind speaking tours in January, and in February the Los Angeles Chamber of Commerce sponsored a luncheon for the State Park Commission. The meeting was attended by representatives of some 200 civic organizations, women's clubs, nature clubs, and chambers of commerce from throughout southern California. Prospects were bright and enthusiasm so great that a more ambitious campaign strategy was soon devised. Rather than a relatively low-budget effort focused around a few special events, an all-out "saturation campaign" was planned.

Leaflets and windshield stickers were designed, printed, and mailed; local campaign committees were formed; endorsements were sought from individuals and groups throughout the state; a constant stream of press releases, feature stories, photographs, and cartoon suggestions was sent to newspapers throughout the state; a speakers bureau was formed and "lantern slides" and motion picture shorts were prepared.

Distinguished individuals who gave generously of their time as speakers on behalf of the bond issue included Duncan McDuffie, William Colby, Colonel Wing, Fred G. Stevenot, director of the newly created Department of Natural Resources, and Newton Drury. A number of academicians including

Ralph Chaney, Willis Linn Jepson, and William F. Badé also made valuable contributions to the campaign as knowledgeable and persuasive speakers. A special, month-long speaking tour of southern California was carried out by Winfield Scott, a longtime member of the Calaveras Grove Association. Scott's time and travel expenses were paid by the National Lumbermen's Association.

In March, at the request of the State Park Commission and its chairman, Will Colby, the California Development Association sponsored an all-day meeting of northern California civic leaders and park enthusiasts. At this meeting, held in San Francisco and attended by some 300 people, Colby was able

to announce the creation of a new state park on the slopes of Mount Tamalpais. A deep, stream-filled canyon thick with redwoods and known as Steep Ravine had been donated to the state in the hope, Colby said, that the area would ultimately become part of a far larger park on the slopes of the mountain. This generous gift had been made a few days earlier by William Kent, just hours before his death. It was, as Colby pointed out, one of the very last acts of a man who had long been associated with the conservation movement. As the donor of Muir Woods National Monument, as a close personal friend of Stephen T. Mather, and as principal author of the legislation that created the National Park Service, Kent had

been closely associated with national park matters. Nevertheless, he had felt that Steep Ravine and the rest of Mount Tamalpais could best be administered as a *state* park. His magnificent 200-acre gift, therefore, had been made to the State Park System and to the people of California.

In April, Roland Vandegrift of the California Taxpayers Association addressed a letter to the State Parks Council in which he described "very frankly" his organization's reservations about the upcoming bond act and the problems of cost that might arise from any ambitious state park program. Drury and other park supporters had been expecting some kind of opposition from the Taxpayers Association, and so they took Vandegrift's question-filled letter very seriously. Drawing upon his experience as a student of rhetoric and public debate. Drury responded carefully and fully to Vandegrift's 14 questions. The result was a document that came to be very popular among campaign workers.

Vandegrift questioned the impact of removing real estate from local tax rolls. Drury replied that most state park acquisition in California would take place in relatively remote areas where tax implications would be minimal. He pointed out, with an example or two, that the creation of parks in other states had tended to increase adjacent land values and thereby replace or even increase tax income to local governments.

Vandegrift questioned the wisdom of setting a precedent by using bond funds for park acquisition. Drury responded that California was being very modest with its $6 million proposal, and was far behind other states in such funding efforts. In the previous fifteen years New York had issued $26.5 million in state park bonds; the City of Chicago and Cook County in Illinois had issued $17.5 million; Illinois was soon to vote on $20 million worth of state park bonds; a similar issue in Pennsylvania was on the ballot for $25 million.

Vandegrift opposed bond issues in general because they involved the payment of interest. He asked if it would not be better for the state to acquire parks on a pay-as-you-go basis. Drury replied that the funds needed for park acquisition were not immediately

Ralph Yardley cartoon in the Stockton Record, *July 21, 1928.*

NATIONAL MEET ON STATE PARKS PLANNED AT BAY

Shall It Be This?   . . . Or This?

Executives of State Playgrounds to Come From All Over Nation

available in the state treasury. Moreover, stretching the payment over thirty years was reasonable because future generations would share in the benefits of the park program. Besides, he pointed out, unlike a building, a highway, or other public works, parks were an appreciating asset—worth far more in future than at the time of acquisition.

To Vandegrift's query about the total cost—principal and interest—of the park bonds, Drury replied that it came to about four cents per person per year.

Drury also reminded Vandegrift that the $6 million in state bond funds would be matched by local and private funds including about $1.5 million already promised from people outside California. Could the voters, Drury asked, "afford to lose these generous offers of private gifts?

"The benefit to California will be many times the cost. State parks will pay not only in increased revenue and population for the state but, what is more important, will pay rich dividends in the health and happiness of our peo-

ple by assuring for them and for their successors, enjoyment of the scenic beauty and outdoor recreation which Californians have always looked upon as their heritage.

"All this for four cents per person per year!"

It was an answer to warm the heart of the most deeply committed fiscal conservative. And although the California Taxpayers Association did not go so far as to endorse the state park bond act, it did decide against an active campaign in opposition.

The most widely celebrated event in the entire campaign occurred in late June and early July when the National Conference on State Parks held its annual meeting in California. Attended by park leaders and enthusiasts from every part of the nation, the meeting got underway on June 26 in the Mark Hopkins Hotel in San Francisco. Stephen T. Mather, founder and chairman of the National Conference, called the meeting to order and introduced the first speaker, Governor C. C. Young.

The governor welcomed the delegates to California and explained that he was supporting the state park bond act even though he generally disapproved of bond acts as a way of financing public works. He cited two justifications for this exception: first of all, he said, the bonds would be used to acquire parks—permanent assets that would only increase in value with the passage of time; second, state expenditures would be matched dollar for dollar by private gifts so that $6 million of public funds would actually acquire $12 million worth of park land. The park bonds were therefore an investment in California's future that was simply too good to pass up.

Other leading speakers of the day included Dr. John C. Merriam, president of the Save-the-Redwoods League and of the Carnegie Institution, J. D. Grant of the Save-the-Redwoods League, and Mather himself. The meeting was well attended and well covered by the press. All of the important speeches were broadcast by KFRC, a major San Francisco radio station.

The second day of the conference was devoted to informal discussion and to a field trip to Mount Tamalpais and Muir Woods National Monument. The more formal program of the conference

Ralph Yardley cartoon in the Stockton Record, *June 1928.*

Rubicon Point and beach at Lake Tahoe.

resumed the following day when Duncan McDuffie presided over a panel of speakers that included several members of the State Park Commission. Commission Chairman Colby echoed the governor's sentiments by describing the State Park System as a worthwhile long term investment. The beauty and significance of Park areas, he said, "is something which, if it is preserved properly, will last forever."

"From an educational standpoint," Dr. Ray Lyman Wilbur of Stanford University said, "our national and state parks should be shrines to which our children go for inspiration and education. Our educational programs have too much been stereotyped along narrow scholastic and academic lines. . . . The state parks offer a great field to the scientist and to the student . . . to learn the early lessons of biology, botany, zoology, meteorology and the effects of the weather upon plant life, directly by observation . . . to learn something of forestry and the physiology and growth of plants, or insect pests and their enemies."

Major Frederick Russell Burnham, one of the founders of the International Boy Scout movement, spoke of the value of parks to young people. "One great heritage we can hand down to the coming generations," he said, "is vast tracts of unspoiled wilderness. We must pass it on to them as we found it, beautiful, austere, awe-inspiring; a place where Man comes close to his Creator. . . . In the old days it was the poor Indian who needed a reservation, but now it is the poor White man who needs a reservation where he can again put his foot on the earth, see the blue sky without smoke, and where children can play on the seashore."

Perhaps the most exciting news to come out of the meeting was an announcement by Colby that the Bliss family of San Francisco was prepared to donate Rubicon Point and approximately one and one-half miles of scenic shoreline property at Lake Tahoe to the State Park System. The 162-acre gift would honor the memory of Duane L. Bliss, a pioneer developer of the Tahoe area. As Colby put it, the gift would constitute the "splendid nucleus" of a very fine state park, provided the voters approved the park bond issue in November.

Colby also described other potential gifts that depended upon passage of the bond issue. Several redwood groves would undoubtedly come into state park ownership through the Save-the-Redwoods League, he said, if the bonds were approved. And Colby also reminded his audience that President Coolidge had just signed federal legislation (April 14, 1928) turning over 1,200 acres of federally owned forestland between the north and south Calaveras Groves—the gift to be effective if and when either or both groves were acquired by the State of California for park purposes.

On Friday, June 29, many delegates to the conference "motored" to Mount Diablo, drove south to Big Basin to see California Redwood Park, or took the train north to inspect potential park areas in the north coast redwood region. On the following Monday, July 2, formal proceedings of the conference resumed in the Chamber of Commerce Building in Los Angeles with chamber executive C. J. S. Williamson presiding.

Keynote speaker for the Los Angeles portion of the National Conference was Stephen Mather. He was supported by members of the State Park Commission and others, including Duncan McDuffie, Major William A. Welch of Palisades Interstate Park of New York, and by Colonel Richard Lieber, who had blazed the way for park advocates in Indiana and whose contagious idealism had made him a leading figure in the park movement all across the nation.

Throughout the campaign, Newton Drury traveled extensively around the state, meeting with newspaper publishers, chamber of commerce leaders, and other groups and individuals whose endorsement would be especially important.

In September and October the campaign reached full magnitude, and endorsement of the bond issue was virtually universal. Almost every newspaper in the state had come out in favor of the bonds, as had some 250 organizations including the California Development Association, chambers of commerce in cities and counties throughout the state, the American Legion, the auto clubs, conservation and education groups, the California Real Estate Association, the State Federation of Women's Clubs, garden clubs both local and national, the Native Sons and

Daughters of the Golden West, the Redwood Empire Association, and various tourist and travel associations.

Feature stories and editorials in support of the bond issue appeared in hundreds of newspapers and magazines. The *Saturday Evening Post,* for example, published a very favorable story that reached some 250,000 subscribers in California alone. The *New York Times* did an editorial so glowing that it was subsequently reprinted as campaign literature. A full page pictorial story appeared in the *San Francisco Chronicle.* And, thanks to G. Elmer Reynolds, editor of the *Stockton Record* and a longtime friend of the park movement, pictorial stories, cartoons, and editorials appeared almost weekly in the *Record's* unique "Out-o-Doors" section.

Once proposition numbers were assigned to the issues on the November ballot, the campaign became simpler. Leaflets, flyers, stationery, and other materials all bore the message: "Vote YES on Amendment Number 4." At roughly the same time it was learned that no argument against the bond issue had been submitted for use on the ballot. Proposition 4 was officially "unopposed."

In the last weeks of the campaign, approximately one million leaflets were distributed by local chambers of commerce, utility companies, and other organizations. The Boy Scouts in southern California and the Campfire Girls in northern California were especially helpful in this aspect of the campaign.

Radio announcements and editorials favoring the bond act were sponsored by major oil companies, by the California Farm Bureau Federation, and by other groups and individuals. Film star Mary Pickford had her studio produce and distribute a motion picture "short" featuring state park scenes and calling for a YES vote on Proposition 4. The film was shown in movie theaters throughout California during the last days of the campaign.

At the polls on November 6, 1928, despite lingering disillusionment with bond issues in general, the people of California voted overwhelmingly in favor of the California State Park Bond issue. The exact tally on Proposition 4 was 346,998 votes no; 975,979 votes yes—a plurality of nearly three to one.

Large-scale public works projects were the order of the day in the 1930s. The San Francisco-Oakland Bay Bridge was completed and opened to public use November 12, 1936. At the time of this photo the bridge was nearing completion, the transbay ferries were still running, and despite economic hard times the cities of the Bay Area were rapidly assuming their modern appearance. Then as now, Mount Diablo rose above it all, majestically dominating the eastern horizon.

6 Building the System

"There is nothing so American as our parks. The scenery and wildlife are native. The fundamental idea behind the parks is native. It is, in brief, that the country belongs to the people.... Parks stand as the outward symbol of this great human principle."

Franklin Delano Roosevelt

Cartoon by "Ket" in the Oakland Tribune, *November 10, 1928.*

After the Election

The State Park Bond Act of 1928 was a milestone in the history of the California State Park System. Yet, for those who were most vitally involved at the time, it was not a moment that called for a great round of celebration. There was considerable elation, of course. But the bond act was simply enabling legislation. In a sense, everything that had been accomplished by the state park movement up to and including voter approval of the bond act was only preparation for the truly great accomplishments that now seemed imminent. Therefore, rather than taking time to savor the election results, leaders of the state park movement quietly set to work building the system.

The state parks had a total estimated value of just over $1 million dollars as of January 1929. There were a dozen parks and five historic monuments in the system. And only one of these areas, California Redwood Park in Big Basin, was heavily visited or much developed for public use. Some of the other parks were so small and so lacking in facilities that they could be used only for strolling and informal picnicking. Overnight camping was possible in the highway-related north coast redwood parks, though by far the most popular and usable of these areas was Richardson Grove, which was entirely in the hands of a concessionaire and had been developed entirely with private money.

Some of the parks were totally unusable. The 639-acre state park high atop Mount Diablo, for example, was completely surrounded by private land. To reach the "park" one had to obtain a permit from the adjacent land owners. And there were other kinds of problems throughout the system. Fire suppression capability in most of the parks was virtually nonexistent. Water supplies and sanitary facilities were either lacking or inadequate. Even the facilities at California Redwood Park were grossly inadequate for the number of visitors that poured into the park on summer weekends. Park staff housing was generally nonexistent. Boundaries were unsurveyed and trespass by adjacent property owners, loggers, and hunters was difficult if not impossible to control.

The state historic monuments had long been neglected, a situation complicated by the state park legislation of 1927 that expressly prohibited the Division of Parks from acquiring or operating state parks within the limits of incorporated cities. Until the legislation could be amended, Sonoma Mission, the Monterey monuments, and Sutter's Fort remained under the jurisdiction of the Department of Finance. Colton Hall and the Custom House in Monterey, and the Marshall Museum or "Blacksmith Shop" in the little town of Kelsey, were even more deeply lost in administrative limbo because the state did not own them and the leases had all been allowed to lapse.

Fifteen people made up the entire field staff of the Division of Parks: there were seven seasonal employees and five general-assistance laborers. A resident custodian looked after Pio Pico Mansion in the south, and there were two "state park wardens," one to look after the north coast redwood parks and the other in charge of California Redwood Park in Big Basin. State Park System headquarters was a two-room office in the Mills Building in San Francisco. Three people worked there: Colonel Charles B. Wing, Chief of the Division; Laura E. Gregory, the very able Secretary to the State Park Commission; and Alice M. Garibaldi, a secretary-stenographer. There was no accountant or bookkeeper. Payroll and other fiscal services were all provided by the Department of Natural Resources. There was no landscape architect or park planner. All such services were to be obtained by contract—for the time being, by contract with Frederick Law Olmsted. Total annual expenditures by the Division of Parks and the State Park Commission together came to approximately $63,000.

Although the State Park System of 1928-29 was small and primitive, its prospects were bright. And early in 1929, while the commission and other interested parties were eagerly awaiting publication of the Olmsted State Park Survey, two new developments added still further luster to park system prospects.

In January, representatives of John D. Rockefeller, Jr. notified the Save-the-Redwoods League that the Rockefeller gift of $1 million for park acquisition of Bull Creek-Dyerville Flat need not be

Mount San Jacinto.

kept anonymous and secret any longer. Voter approval of the State Park Bond Act had convinced Rockefeller that Californians were ready to shoulder their own local responsibilities with regard to redwood forest preservation and related state park matters. Rockefeller now informed the league that he was ready and willing to donate another $1 million for redwood preservation purposes if the amount could be matched by other private donors. As a result of this decision by Rockefeller, the league made a public announcement in March 1929 that Rockefeller had given $1 million to the cause of state redwood parks. Announcement of Rockefeller's offer to provide another million dollars was delayed pending the organization of a full-scale campaign designed to raise the required matching money.

At almost the same time it was learned that newly elected President Herbert Hoover had selected a member of the State Park Commission to serve in his administration as Secretary of the Interior. Dr. Ray Lyman Wilbur would be leaving his post as president of Stanford University to accept the appointment. This meant that the California State Park movement would have a powerful new ally in a key position in Washington. Hoover himself was an alumnus of Stanford and had other strong ties to California. He could be counted on to be sympathetic to California state park interests.

Olmsted and the State Park Survey

During 1928 Frederick Law Olmsted was busy with a number of other projects on the west coast and elsewhere about the nation. He nevertheless accepted the State Park Survey assignment and managed to meet the December 31 deadline specified in his contract. But in order to do this he found it necessary to plunge into the survey work with even more than his customary enthusiasm and devotion.

He worked long hours. He traveled extensively. He conferred and corresponded with dozens of people from all parts of the State. Drury later characterized Olmsted's commitment to the survey as "heroic."

"Olmsted," he said, "was not physically a big man . . . but he was a man of tremendous vitality. He was a terrier. He never left a problem until he'd gotten out of it everything there was to get. He'd work all hours of the night, and he could work just as well in the back seat of an automobile as he could in an office on Park Avenue in New York."

Olmsted's field notes, letters, site reports and other written materials were likely to be written out whenever circumstances permitted and on whatever scrap of paper was handy. "I don't get much time for writing by day," he once explained to Laura Gregory, "except scratching notes for my own use." But at night, or while traveling, the ideas would begin to fly, and the words would go down in a tiny, fast-moving scrawl—on scratch pads, graph paper, hotel stationery, anything—for he had the ability to lose himself in his work, to become so engrossed that he would hardly notice what was going on around him.

The ideas, the vision that he brought to his work, were similar to those of his father. He was perhaps more patient with governmental complexities, more tolerant of other points of view. But he shared his father's great respect for the future and concern for the welfare of society as a whole.

Olmsted also brought other qualities to his work that were both charming and of considerable practical value. He was a gentleman: gracious, polite, unassuming, unpretentious. Though he was independent in his thinking, he was nevertheless sensitive to psychological, philosophical, and aesthetic subtleties. Committed to and preoccupied with lofty concepts, he was nevertheless quick to deal with legal, economic and political complexities.

Olmsted's total immersion in his work had two results by the end of 1928: he turned in the typescript of his state park survey report on December 31st—and went into the hospital with painful symptoms brought on by overwork.

The report was a great success! It did far more than simply list a number of possible park projects and set them in priority according to the political expediencies of the moment. Olmsted based his recommendations on his own long-range view of the public wel-

fare, and on legal grounds as stated in the constitution of the United States of America. State parks, according to Olmsted, were an important tool whereby state government could help make a reality out of the constitutionally guaranteed right of all Americans to the pursuit of happiness. The enjoyment of natural scenery and participation in non-urban outdoor recreation, Olmsted pointed out, "have always been part of the joy of living for many people. But in our time, in America, there has been an enormous increase in the proportion of people who have time left for the pursuit of such values after earning the bare necessities of existence."

The extent of this interest in natural scenery and outdoor recreation could be estimated by adding up the vast amounts of money spent in California for such things as travel for pleasure. Money spent on hotels, resorts, camps, eating places, stores, vacation homes, scenic highways, and scenic railways in localities where people went for the purpose of enjoying outdoor life—all this could be added up and calculated. But, Olmsted pointed out: "How far such values *can* be bought, at any price, by succeeding generations in California will depend largely on the degree to which the physical conditions which make them possible are conserved or are destroyed by the first comers through their wasteful methods of exploiting them." It was the responsibility of government, Olmsted said, to put scenic and recreational resources on a "sustained yield" basis just as it had in the case of timber resources.

If the beauty and charm and outdoor recreational opportunities of the state were not to be wasted, two things were necessary: "(1) *to teach the great mass of well-intentioned people how to get what they want* in enjoyment of scenic and recreational values, *how to get it successfully* for themselves now and on their own initiative, and *how to get it without destroying the natural assets* on which the continued enjoyment of such values depends; and (2) *to curb and limit the activities of exploiters* who would destroy the birthright of their successors, no matter what its value, for the sake of a quick turn of profit to themselves."

In order to act on these urgent con-

State Park Warden Everett E. Powell in Big Sur State Park about 1936. The designation "ranger" was not yet in use. Standard uniform regulations were not yet in effect.

cerns, Olmsted concluded, the state should prepare a comprehensive plan for the preservation and development of scenic and recreational resources. Once available, the plan should be used as the basis of a broad program of conservation education designed to let everyone know what was at stake, and what measures might be needed in order to protect and enhance scenic and recreational resources in the state. Olmsted also recommended that the state take direct steps to prevent "unwarrantably destructive exploitation of important scenic and recreational resources." This could be accomplished to a large extent by the intelligent use of planning and zoning techniques. It might also be necessary and advisable in special cases to acquire or exercise proprietary control. Scenic easements, for example, might be acquired alongside highways in order to protect roadside scenery without destroying economically valuable forestry or agricultural activities.

Olmsted identified three truly great opportunities to preserve and enhance publicly owned scenic and recreational values: (1) the tidelands along the seashore; (2) the shorelines of rivers and lakes; and (3) state highway rights-of-way. The rivers, riverside highways, and riverside flood control devices of the central valley, for example, could provide tremendous opportunities for scenic enjoyment and healthful outdoor recreation "for an expenditure quite trifling in money alongside of all that has been spent and will be spent on unavoidable public improvements."

Olmsted indicated that he and his assistants had investigated some 330 potential park sites on the recommendation of various groups and individuals. Some of these sites they had found to be too small, or too isolated, or too local in their appeal; others were too expensive in relation to their park potential and the availability of similar sites. But even after a rigorous process of elimination, Olmsted was left with 125 sites that he felt were fully deserving of state park status. If these sites could be acquired, and if other less threatened sites could be acquired later, an excellent State Park System could be developed. But, as Olmsted himself pointed out, not all of the 125 recommended sites could be acquired

by the state "without spending several times the $6 million of the present bond issue. . . ." It was going to be necessary to set up a priority system and make some hard decisions.

Olmsted recommended that park projects be selected from each of several categories. Sea coast projects were divided into several geographical subdivisions; redwood forest projects were divided north and south; a special category was set up for giant sequoia areas in the Sierra Nevada. Special categories were also set up for parks that might take advantage of scenic features such as lakes, rivers, or mountains. Projects of historical or scientific interest were a separate category, as were desert projects.

The vast southern California desert, Olmsted said, deserved special attention, not so much to preserve well-known or spectacular scenic features as to preserve a unique intellectual and emotional opportunity: "Certain desert areas have a distinctive and subtle charm in part dependent on spaciousness, solitude, and escape from the evidence of human control and manipulation of the earth, a charm of constantly growing value as the rest of the earth becomes more completely dominated by man's activities." This distinctive and subtle charm, Olmsted indicated, could be "easily destroyed by comparatively slight changes made by man," and so it was important for the state to "preserve inviolate several desert areas large enough for future generations to enjoy in perfection the essential desert qualities. As in the case of the ancient redwood forests, only such public action by the present generation on an adequate scale can preserve this heritage for the people of centuries to come."

Favorable comment began to come in even while the report was still in typescript, and requests for printed copies were received from all over California and other parts of the nation. But the highest kind of praise for Olmsted's report lies in the fact that it set the tone and direction of State Park System development from that time forward. As rarely happens to masterplans and other large-scale public planning documents, almost every specific recommendation in the Olmsted report has been followed.

On a more general and philosophical level, it might be argued that government as a whole—local, state, and national—has not lived up to Olmsted's vision of its responsibility to preserve and develop scenic and outdoor recreational opportunity for present and future generations. Of course, the story is not over. American society continues to revise and reshape itself. And relatively recent events in California—the California Coastal Act, for example, or the gradual development of educational and interpretive programs in parks and in schools—continue to give promise to the possibility that we may yet more fully achieve the broad social and environmental goals that Olmsted described in his report.

Meanwhile, state park rangers, park visitors, and park enthusiasts of all kinds tend to feel that they are participating in a program of noble intent. This sense of purpose, this day-to-day commitment to what is sometimes called the "state park ethic," can be traced in large part to the broad vision, clear logic, and practical idealism of Frederick Law Olmsted and the California State Park Survey of 1928.

Acquisition

Early in 1929 as the State Park Commission began to wrestle with the complexities of acquisition matters, it became apparent that the matching requirement built into the bond act

William E. Colby
about 1934.

might cause a great deal of trouble unless someone could be found to direct the program who had both a thorough understanding of park matters and diplomatic ability of a high order. Persuading people to come up with matching funds was not going to be easy. Will Colby and others had assumed that Olmsted could be counted on to lead the way in such matters. But Olmsted was not available. He was out of the hospital and able to work, but his doctors had ordered him to take it very easy. Colby, Olmsted, and others therefore began to look toward Newton Drury. He had already proven his ability in a similar role with the Save-the-Redwoods League. He would be ideal for the state park acquisition job if he could be persuaded to accept it.

In a letter to Colby dated January 29, 1929, Olmsted described the situation: "The Commission should have a man of very broad grasp in constant and complete charge of the acquirement program, a man of Mr. Drury's calibre if any way obtainable." A few days later, Colby informed Olmsted that the commission had indeed asked Drury to undertake the acquisition program and that he was considering the matter. "If we can secure his service," Colby wrote, "it will be a great relief because through long contact with Mr. Drury we know we can rely absolutely upon his representations. Further, he knows his limitations as well as anyone else and will not advise us beyond a point where

he knows his ground is certain." The strategy would be to have Drury handle everything about the program right up to the point where Olmsted's accumulated wisdom about park and landscape matters would be of most value. Then, it was hoped, Olmsted could be called upon to confer with Drury, perhaps make some field inspections, and otherwise help the commission determine the optimal size and shape of various park proposals.

In February, Drury agreed to work part-time for the commission as "investigating officer" in charge of acquisition matters. The rest of his time would be spent on fund raising and acquisition for the Save-the-Redwoods League. Since the two assignments were inter-related in crucial ways, the arrangement was fortunate from every point of view. Soon Drury and Olmsted were in close touch, conferring at length and agreeing on a general strategy for the acquisition program.

With Olmsted's approval, Drury edited, selected illustrations for, and otherwise prepared the survey report for publication. He also followed through on a number of gifts to the park system that had been promised during the bond act campaign including 162 acres of forestland at Rubicon Point overlooking Lake Tahoe. This spectacularly scenic area had a cash value in excess of $82,000 and was a gift to the people of California from the heirs of Duane L. Bliss, a pioneer lumberman and resort developer at the lake. In February and March, the Save-the-Redwoods League turned over six parcels of redwood forestland to the State Park System. These magnificent redwood groves—600 acres in all, worth about $77,000 in monetary terms—had been acquired by the league through the generosity of many individuals, notably Mrs. Harris Whittemore and family, and Mrs. Perry Stout, wife of the president of the Del Norte Lumber Company. The Bliss family gift was eventually matched by state funds, but the stunning generosity of the league and its donors was already beginning to outstrip the state's ability to respond.

Later in 1929, legislative appropriations made it possible to enlarge the state's holdings at Richardson Grove, and to acquire an estimated ten miles of shoreline at Mission Bay near San

Diego. In November, another state appropriation made it possible to match funds provided by the Tamalpais Conservation Club for acquisition of 520 acres of land at Mount Tamalpais adjacent to Steep Ravine—the area William Kent had given to the State Park System.

The first sale and use of state park bond funds occurred in October 1929 when Drury was finally able to complete some rather complex negotiations involving 390 acres at Patrick's Point in Humboldt County. Matching funds for this acquisition were provided by the Save-the-Redwoods League; special assistance in the negotiations was provided by Arthur E. Connick, who had been appointed to the State Park Commission in March 1929. Connick had long been associated with the league and his appointment to the commission by Governor Young was a very sound move. Well known in California banking circles, Connick was intimately familiar with the economics of the north coast redwood region and held the respect and trust of both lumber interests and park advocates.

In 1930, new acreage was added to Del Norte Coast Redwoods, Mount Tamalpais, Bliss-Rubicon and other already established state parks. But the major new acquisitions that year were in southern California: 12,695 acres at Mount San Jacinto, and approximately one mile of sandy beach alongside the ocean at Santa Monica. This beach acquisition troubled some observers because it required such a large expenditure of funds—$1 million in state park bond funds matched by $1 million worth of land given to the state by Los Angeles County. Yet the beach was easily accessible to a very large population and promised to be a heavily used, extremely popular addition to the State Park System. Political advice, leadership, and various kinds of practical assistance on this and other southern California acquisitions were provided by State Park Commissioner Henry W. O'Melveny, perhaps the best-known and most highly admired attorney in southern California at the time.

Connick was very active on north coast acquisition matters, and O'Melveny paid special attention to beach and other southern California park acquisitions, but it was Will Colby who,

The State Park Commission about 1934. Left to right: William T. Hart, Joseph R. Knowland, P. E. Hatch, Mrs. Edmund N. "Madie" Brown, William E. Colby.

as chairman of the commission, looked after the statewide program. Colby had agreed to chair the commission provided the office of the Division of Parks could be located conveniently close to his own office in the Mills Building in downtown San Francisco. Once this arrangement was made, however, it seemed only natural that *all* important matters should be brought to him for advice and final approval. As a result, for several years, Colby spent at least half of his work time on park matters.

Colby's parks commitment caused him to neglect his law practice, but he enjoyed the work so much that he later described his years on the park commission as "a wonderful time, one of the happiest experiences of my whole life." It was, he said many years later, a rare opportunity for great accomplishment "because conditions were just perfect when we took over the new commission and began to purchase park lands under the bond issue." The people, the legislature, and the governor were generally supportive. And the commission was made up of extraordinarily capable men, all of whom were genuinely interested in state park matters. This favorable situation remained in effect throughout the administration of Governor C. C. Young, and continued with relatively little change after

January 6, 1931, when Young was replaced as governor by the colorful, longtime mayor of San Francisco, James "Sunny Jim" Rolph.

Even the stock market crash of October 1929, and the subsequent depression, did not greatly disturb the state park acquisition program of the early 1930s. In fact, it might be argued that depressed land and timber values led to some of the great park accomplishments of that time. Clearly the major acquisitions of 1931 would not have come about if housing construction and commercial subdivision activity had been prospering, and if lumber had therefore been in greater demand.

The first great acquisition accomplishment of 1931—the Bull Creek and Dyerville Flats—had been years in the making. Negotiations between park advocates and the Pacific Lumber Company concerning the great old redwood forest in those areas had been stalled since 1925, and Pacific Lumber's asking price had ranged upward to $10 million and more. Now, Drury, Connick, Colby, McDuffie, and other leaders of the Save-the-Redwoods League were at last able to negotiate a settlement with Pacific Lumber and adjacent owners. The agreement included thirteen parcels of land, 13,629 acres, for a total of $3.2 million. The state put up $1.8

million in bond funds, and the league matched that amount with a combination of land and money. This meant that through the generosity of John D. Rockefeller, Jr. and others, the league had accomplished one of its primary objectives. And the people of the state and nation had acquired one of the scenic wonders of the world.

There were also other major acquisitions in 1931. Half a mile of southern California beach frontage valued at more than $100,000 was donated to the park system by Edward L. Doheny. This and other gifts of land—mostly from private developers caught short by depressed market conditions—were used to match state park bond funds. San Clemente Beach in San Diego County, Morro Strand in San Luis Obispo County, and Seacliff and Sunset Beaches in Santa Cruz County were acquired in this way. Acquisitions at Manhattan Beach, Carpinteria, and Silver Strand involved either cash or land contributions from county governments in Los Angeles, Santa Barbara, and San Diego Counties. The North Grove at Calaveras Big Trees was acquired with matching funds provided largely by the Save-the-Redwoods League, thus ending more than thirty years of frustration on the part of the Calaveras Grove Association and others who had long been striving to preserve that famous old grove of giant sequoias.

Eight miles of toll road were acquired at Mount Diablo along with some 900 acres of land—the first portion of a five-year-long, parcel-by-parcel acquisition agreement that would eventually create a 2,000-acre state park surrounding the top of the mountain. This acquisition was made possible by $70,000 in matching funds from the people of Contra Costa County. Cash contributions from San Diego County—ultimately amounting to more than $50,000— made it possible to acquire approximately 1,600 acres of land at Palomar Mountain. Several existing parks including Prairie Creek and Mill Creek Redwoods State Parks (now Jedediah Smith Redwoods State Park), and Bliss-Rubicon State Park at Lake Tahoe, were significantly enlarged during 1931.

Total acquisition expenditures for the year approached $6 million, of which $2.9 million came out of bond funds. About 14 miles of ocean beach had

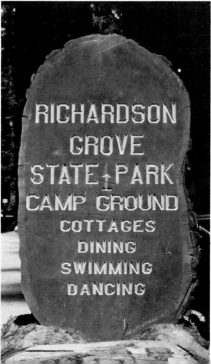

Richardson Grove State Park entrance sign and river scenery. One of the most popular parks in the system during the 1930s.

Point Lobos State Reserve as it appeared during the early 1930s.

been added to the park system, and total park acreage was nearly doubled. These expenditures, and others already in the planning stage, meant that acquisition funds were in increasingly short supply from this time onward. In order to maintain statewide balance in the acquisition program using the limited funds that were still available, some wonderful opportunities had to be turned down. The South Grove at Calaveras Big Trees, for example, was offered to the state at a bargain price. But as Colby, Drury, and others reluctantly agreed, it was simply impossible to consider any additional projects without threatening to disrupt the overall program.

Some 20,000 acres of pine forest and rolling meadowland high in the Laguna Mountains east of San Diego were acquired in 1933 when Ralph M. Dyar donated half of the appraised value of "Rancho Cuyamaca." At roughly the same time, prolonged negotiations regarding Point Lobos reached a turning point.

Olmsted considered Point Lobos absolutely the most important scenic and scientific preservation project on the entire coast of California. The area was world famous, but was still privately owned despite a persistent campaign for public acquisition led by Mrs. Robert Hunter and the Point Lobos Association. Matching funds for state park acquisition purposes simply did not seem to be available. The problem had haunted Drury for months. Then, one night just as he was dozing off, he found himself suddenly wide awake with a possible answer.

Through the instrumentality of the Save-the-Redwoods League, Edward S. Harkness of New York had given

a half-million dollars to the State of California for redwood forestland acquisition at Prairie Creek. The state had never matched that particular gift. Would it be possible, Drury wondered, to use that excess matching credit to authorize the use of bond funds for acquisition of Point Lobos? The State Attorney General's office was queried. A favorable opinion was obtained. And shortly afterward, the state was able to acquire 400 acres of land at Point Lobos.

The price was high: $631,000. But the wild beauty of the area was unique. Francis McComas, a student of landscape and a painter of renown, once described Point Lobos as "the greatest meeting of land and water in the world." Today that sentiment is no doubt shared by untold numbers of people, for literally millions have visited Point Lobos State Reserve since its creation in 1933.

Longtime advocates of desert preservation were also cheered during this period by progress toward the creation of a large state park in the desert region of southern California. By the time the State Park System was created in 1927, forlorn homesteads, misguided attempts at agriculture, and various forms of speculative development were already beginning to mar the broad plains, badlands, palm-filled canyons, and high mountains of the southern California desert. Ray Lyman Wilbur had been aware of this problem while still a member of the State Park Commission. After his appointment as Secretary of the Interior in 1929, he put a temporary stop to further "homesteading," mining claims, and other forms of private pre-emption of federal lands in the desert region, pending the development of a long-range park acqui-

sition plan. Then in 1933, at Wilbur's instigation and with help from Colby, Drury, and others, legislation was submitted by Congressman Phil Swing and Senator Hiram Johnson that would enable the State Park System to acquire 189,000 acres of desert land by simply paying the filing fees.

With spirited support from Congressman Swing, Secretary Wilbur, and others—and to the surprise of many—the Johnson-backed senate bill was successfully pushed through Congress in the spring of 1933 and signed by President Franklin Delano Roosevelt. Although several years would elapse before all the details of the filing process could be completed, park supporters were assured that a magnificent desert park, as envisioned in the Olmsted report, would eventually be created around Borrego Valley east of San Diego on the edge of the great Colorado Desert.

Meanwhile, Ellen B. Scripps, George Marston, and other leading citizens of San Diego provided their own personal money for matching purposes and worked closely with Guy Fleming and Newton Drury to bring about State Park System ownership of Borrego Palm Canyon and certain other key parcels of privately owned land in the Borrego region.

Other important acquisitions at this time included Pfeiffer Big Sur, Morro Bay, Armstrong Redwoods, Castle Crags, James D. Phelan Beach in San Francisco, the Sonoma Coast beaches, the plaza and several historic buildings at San Juan Bautista, and the entire valley surrounding the site of the old Spanish mission, La Purisima Concepcion, near Lompoc in Santa Barbara County.

As a result of these and other acqui-

Cuyamaca Peak looking west. Cuyamaca Rancho State Park.

sitions, and additions to existing parks, the State Park System grew from a dozen parks and five historic monuments in 1928 to 49 parks and 11 historic monuments in 1934. Total acreage increased from 13,700 to about 300,000 acres including the federal land at Borrego. Total cash value of all these state park holdings increased from a little over $1 million to more than $14 million. And park visitation increased from about 60,000 in 1928 to nearly six million (including day-use visitors to beach areas) in 1934.

After 1934, however, only minimal growth was possible for the State Park System. By then, the 1928 Park Bond Fund was 95 percent exhausted, and additional funding for acquisition purposes was not feasible while general economic conditions were so depressed.

Development

The wonderful accomplishment and success of the acquisition program under Newton Drury did not extend to other State Park System programs. The creation of new parks, the expansion of old ones, and the great increase in the number of park visitors, all put tremendous stress on park support systems. But, generally speaking, caught in the economic difficulties that continued throughout much of the 1930s, state government was reluctant to spend money on state parks. Each new governor, and top-level appointees in each new administration, tended to start out with the fervent hope that state parks could be made to pay for themselves, thereby helping to reduce the overall cost of state government.

Parks, it was often said, should be operated on a more "business-like" basis. This could and should be accomplished by increasing user fees and by obtaining more income from more revenue-producing concession contracts. "Mature" and "over-mature" timber in the parks could be sold off and harvested instead of being "wasted." Grazing rights could be sold to the highest bidder. The parks could also be opened up to mineral exploration and mining. Costs could be reduced by keeping park areas closed to the public. If necessary, some parks, or at least parts of them, could be sold outright and the money put back in the general fund.

Such ideas, along with drastic budget-cut proposals, were likely to come from the governor's office early in the tenure of each new administration. Proposals to dismantle the park program also occasionally came from members of the legislature, usually in response to pressure from the California Taxpayers Association or other anti-government-spending groups. In 1933, for example, a senate "fact-finding committee" recommended that the State Park System budget for the next two fiscal years be cut from $279,046 to $100,000. The committee announced that it was making this recommendation because it considered recreation "one of the least essential activities of state government."

Responding to this particular challenge in March 1933, Colonel Wing pointed out that the Division of Parks was already severely understaffed, that only 18 state parks could be kept open to the public with existing staff, and that 29 others were already completely inoperative. Wing also argued that the

state parks were "not a luxury, but an essential part of the life and attractiveness of the state." They contributed significantly to economic activity by encouraging tourism, and contributed perhaps even more importantly to the general welfare by providing opportunities for recreation and relief from the stress of trying times.

Luckily for the State Park System, the recommendations of the 1933 fact-finding committee were rejected. The Division of Parks, after all, had many friends both in and outside state government who could be counted on to defend the system from unreasonable attack. But the early 1930s were difficult years economically, and so it is not surprising that State Park System budgets were extremely lean throughout that time. In 1933, to use that year for an example once again, the Division of Parks' request for 27 new employees and increased administrative funding was rejected by the legislature. As a result, many parks remained off-limits to the public. Even in those parks that were open for public use, trails, camping and picnicking facilities, water and sewage systems, as well as other provisions for the health, safety, and comfort of the visiting public remained generally inadequate or nonexistent. Park system employees simply did the best they could: for three or four months of the year they met the public and kept the parks clean and functional; the rest of the time they designed and built whatever they could to better meet the growing demand for park facilities.

Ironically, the hard times that led to budget problems for the park system also led directly to state park development on an unprecedented scale—to a construction and improvement program

La Purisima Mission
prior to restoration.

carried on over a period of years that many still look upon as the golden era of park development.

The Civilian Conservation Corps

The stock market crash had been a disaster for some and a warning for everyone. The economic difficulties of the next year or two were even harder to ignore. Banks and businesses failed. Manufacturing slowed to 40 percent of capacity. Unemployment was widespread and continued to worsen. Fear, anger, and despair were virtually universal. The spectre of starvation loomed large in the popular imagination.

On November 8, 1932, the people of the nation voted overwhelmingly for a "New Deal." The Democratic majority in Congress was increased, and President Hoover was replaced by Franklin Delano Roosevelt, who said he knew how to get the nation's economy moving again. In his inaugural address of March 4, 1933, Roosevelt described the economic situation as an emergency, one that should be taken as seriously as any conceivable military emergency. The time had come, he said, to mobilize the federal government behind a direct attack on economic problems, "treating the task as we would treat the emergency of war...." Within a week of taking office, Roosevelt had met with his top-level administrators, drawn up an official battleplan, and asked Congress for the necessary legal and financial tools with which to proceed.

In its turn, Congress also moved swiftly. Along with a rush of other legislation, congressional approval was given to an act entitled "Emergency Conservation Work," which provided "for the relief of unemployment through the performance of useful public work, and for other purposes." This bill was signed by the president on March 31, and an executive order was issued April 5, appointing a director of Emergency Conservation Work, transferring $10 million for his use, and creating an advisory council made up of all the agencies that would have a role in the program. The army would set up the camps and provide administrative and logistical support. The Department of Labor would handle recruiting. Technical supervision of the projects would be provided by the Departments of Agriculture and Interior. By July, just four months after inauguration day, nearly 300,000 men were enrolled and work was underway in some 1,330 camps scattered all across the nation.

Technically these were ECW—Emergency Conservation Work—camps, but the term President Roosevelt used in his speech to Congress—"civilian conservation corps"—was the name that took hold. New legislation in 1937 finally made it the official name of the organization. By whatever name it was known, however, the Civilian Conservation Corps was in fact an army of young men—18 to 23 years of age, unmarried, unemployed—who agreed to work for a dollar a day plus room and board, fighting dust storms and forest fires, building fire and flood prevention facilities, planting forests, and improving public parks all across the nation. Many "enrollees" did not know very much about manual labor, but they were willing to learn, eager for an opportunity to show what they could do, and willing to accept the idea that satisfaction in a job well done was the real reward for doing it. As a condition of their enrollment, most of what they earned was sent home to help support their families.

While they helped their families, worked hard, and earned little money, CCC enrollees were learning a lot. Ten percent of the workforce was made up of skilled craftsmen who could provide practical, on-the-job instruction for the less experienced. Beyond that, each CCC camp also featured a library and an education program through which an enrollee could further improve himself. Reading, writing, arithmetic, bookkeeping, automobile repair, and other practical subjects were taught during the evenings after the regular work day. And by means of various university extension programs, high school and college credits could be earned.

Even more vital to the spirit of the CCC, however, was the thorough educational effort that went into each and every job the CCC undertook. The basic assumption was simple: Americans were a proud and independent people. They were used to working on their own initiative. If the enrollees were to work well and efficiently, they would have to understand what each project was all about—its significance to the local community, present and future; its economic value to the people; its recreational value and influence; and enough about the work techniques to be employed that every individual could see how his particular task fit into the overall effort. Great emphasis was placed on the value of teamwork and cooperation. And so each new job began with a company meeting at which the project was described. The superintendent explained every aspect of the work to be done. Blueprints, sketches, photographs, and even scale models were kept on display for continuing reference.

The result of this approach was tremendous esprit-de-corps, and this in turn resulted in a truly amazing record of accomplishment. CCC camps were established in every state of the nation, and enrollees came from every state. For the first time federal, state, county, and metropolitan governments had an adequate supply of labor and funds with which to tackle conservation problems. Forestry, soil conservation, and irrigation and reclamation projects received the greatest attention, along with fire suppression, flood and other emergency relief and rescue programs. But the CCC also did a considerable amount of park development work. Camp and picnic sites were cleared, fireplaces were built, water and sewer systems were developed, firebreaks were cleared, and administration and museum buildings were constructed along with roads, trails, bridges, and other park facilities. Historical restoration projects were also carried out.

Within the California State Park System alone, more than 10,000 man years of labor were put into park development work by the CCC. And many of the more obvious "permanent improvements" that state park visitors find impressive to this day—campstoves, campfire centers, outdoor theaters, buildings and bridges made of stone and other native materials—were the result of this program. Total value of "permanent improvements" to park areas in California was estimated to be several million dollars, even in 1930-1940 terms.

Even the most outspoken critics of FDR and his programs had to admit

Big Basin Redwoods State Park.

that CCC accomplishments were impressive and that the program as a whole was generally very popular. Democrats and Republicans, liberals and conservatives, all endorsed it, and CCC camps were in great demand all across the nation. In California in 1936 a broad-based public opinion poll revealed that nearly everyone approved of the corps and thought it should become a permanent agency of the federal government.

The Works Progress Administration

In 1935, another federal unemployment relief program entered the park development field. The CCC was, after all, just one emergency program among many designed to get the nation's economy moving. In 1935 the umbrella agency for unemployment relief came to be known as the Works Progress Admin-

istration. Its administrator, Harry Hopkins, took on the complex and difficult job of finding meaningful employment for all kinds of people, men and women, young and old, many of whom were not at all suited to manual labor. Many thousands of public employees—school teachers, nurses, librarians, clerical and other technical and professional workers—were unemployed. Because cultural programs were looked upon as luxuries that could not be

Far left: *CCC workers standing proudly beside a four-way "Diablo Stove" at Palomar Mountain State Park, 1935.* Left: *Typical "Diablo Stove" in use.*

justified during hard times, artists, writers, and musicians were also unemployed. The impact of such a pattern of unemployment was an increasingly obvious loss of those benefits that virtually define civilization. The task of the WPA was to reverse that trend.

Regardless of race, religion, age, or sex, the unemployed were to be given opportunities to do whatever they could do best—provided only that the work was "worthwhile" from a public point of view, and not simply the ordinary work that government or industry was already able to do. To guarantee local involvement, understanding, and support, every project had to have a local sponsor. It was also considered essential, just as in the CCC program, that everyone involved in each project should clearly understand the public value of the work being undertaken.

Painters, writers, and musicians gave special attention to American subjects, to large murals in public places, for instance, as opposed to more personal subjects for the private homes and offices of wealthy patrons. WPA-sponsored symphony orchestras, theatrical companies and other art and educational programs also paid special attention to American themes and subjects hoping thereby to bring renewed confidence, self-respect, and vitality to American culture in general. Thousands of school teachers were put back to work, many of them in rural areas where it was calculated that without WPA help more than a million school-age children would have had no schooling. And along with these and many other public service projects, the WPA carried out a great many construction projects including city halls, school buildings, fire houses, public roads, and other civic improvements.

Within the state parks of California, the "boys" of the CCC were eventually outnumbered by WPA enrollees, and many projects were carried out almost interchangeably by these two agencies. In some cases, the WPA was able to provide planning, engineering, and other technical or professional help while the CCC provided the manual labor.

The summit building at Mount Diablo was built in 1938, 1939, and 1940 by CCC enrollees—a special company made up entirely of war veterans. The Standard Oil Company provided $7,500

for building materials as a co-sponsor of the project, which was to be a combination airline-safety beacon, fire lookout tower, public observation platform, and park museum. Plans for the museum were developed under the guidance of a distinguished advisory committee headed by Dr. Bruce L. Clark, a professor of paleontology at the University of California in Berkeley. Historical research as well as exhibit design and construction was coordinated by Rodney S. Ellsworth, a WPA technician assigned to California state park interpretive work. The actual paintings, sketches, diagrams, and other museum exhibits were done by the

WPA-sponsored Federal Art Project in San Francisco. Ironically, this fine example of cooperative endeavor ended in frustration. The elaborate exhibits were never placed on permanent display because the native sandstone, quarried by CCC workers on the lower slopes of the mountain, turned out to be so porous that the building leaked water during and after every rain storm.

An equally ambitious "Pictorial History of Redwoods" was also researched and coordinated by Ellsworth and produced by the San Francisco Art Project for display at Big Basin. This and the Mount Diablo project were looked upon as a practical beginning and stimulus

CCC workers preparing to plaster the walls of the restored church at La Purisima Mission State Historic Park. Below: *CCC model of the main residence building, La Purisima Mission State Historic Park, November 1935. Colby is third from left.*

CCC workers constructing Mountain Theater, Mount Tamalpais State Park.

The Summit Building, Mount Diablo State Park.

for a comprehensive State Park System interpretive program featuring museum exhibits, guided walks, and other interpretive activities. WPA-sponsored guides, for instance, were approved for Mount Diablo. But though all of these programs were very well received by the public, they were not continued by the Division of Parks when federal support was withdrawn and the programs had to compete for funds with other even more fundamental park management matters such as plumbing, wiring, custodial, and public safety work.

In 1937 and 1938, the WPA also funded a state park-related historical research program that resulted in more than 100 monographs or background papers on the state parks and state historic monuments of California. This program, the results of which have proven extremely valuable over the years, was encouraged by Joseph R. Knowland, Aubrey Drury, Herbert Bolton, and others with a special interest in California history. This program was administered by Newton Drury on behalf of the Division of Parks, though the work itself was done in Berkeley at the University of California under the direct supervision of Dr. Aubrey Neasham. Neasham hired competent but needy scholars, many of them postgraduate students of history. As editor and coordinator of the program he saw to it that copies of the final reports were placed in the parks themselves, in the headquarters office of the Division of Parks, and in the Bancroft Library, thus assuring all parties that the information would continue to be easily

available. Several of the 49 or so students who did this research went on to distinguished careers as professional historians, either in the academic world or for governmental agencies including the National Park Service.

Neasham himself left the program in November 1938 in order to become regional historian for the Southwest Region of the National Park Service. But his ties to California were strong, and so both before his temporary departture from the state and later, while on leave-of-absence from the National Park Service, he managed to complete important state park-related historical research projects. He did all of the historical background work for restoration of San Juan Bautista and Columbia State Historic Parks. He also carried out valuable research concerning the Monterey historic monuments and the Custom House, which was finally acquired by the state in June 1938.

The WPA—like the CCC—was criticized by some but praised by many including leading spokesmen from both major political parties in California and across the nation. In 1938, even Governor Frank Merriam of California, a Republican and generally considered a conservative, praised the WPA for its beneficial impact on a troubled economy. And a 1938 survey of city, county, and state officials in California revealed almost universal agreement with Merriam's positive view. Many observers went even further by indicating that they hoped the WPA could be made a permanent public agency. This would be the best way, they argued, to keep

alive the growing patriotism and sense of community generated by WPA programs. The chief spokesman for this point of view was WPA administrator Harry Hopkins himself: "From the very beginning of our national existence, the national government has intervened with all its resources frequently and aggressively in order to develop commerce, agriculture, and industry. Today, while other nations are building vast armaments, we are building parks, libraries, hospitals, and schools on a wartime scale. While other people are learning to use gas masks and bombproof shelters, we are improving the lot of the underprivileged, eliminating illiteracy, opening up opportunities for work and play."

Politics, Oil Royalties, and World War II

During the 1930s—even though great programs of acquisition and development were winning national acclaim for the California State Park System, and the parks themselves were becoming ever more popular and more heavily visited—the State Park Commission and the Division of Parks were beset by increasingly adverse political and economic pressures.

The first State Park Commission had not been troubled by partisan politics. Its members had been selected solely on the basis of merit and proven interest in park and outdoor recreation matters. Nor did the Rolph administration (1931-34) interfere unduly with the

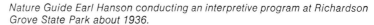

Nature Guide Earl Hanson conducting an interpretive program at Richardson Grove State Park about 1936.

Old Custom House,
Monterey State
Historic Park.

park program for partisan political reasons, although Rolph did insist on the resignation of the banker, Arthur E. Connick, with whom it was said he had had some unfortunate business dealings many years earlier.

Connick's forced and *very* reluctant resignation was sharply protested by many people in California, including some who were close to the governor and who knew how valuable Connick was to the commission, especially in redwood acquisition matters. Commissioners Burnham and O'Melveny came close to resigning in protest. Eventually, however, the matter was smoothed over and an Oakland banker, Joseph F. Carlston, was appointed to the commission in Connick's place. He attended just one meeting before he resigned and was replaced by Joseph R. Knowland, whose experience in public affairs and interest in parks, especially historic parks, made him an extremely valuable addition.

Other changes on the commission during these years included the appointment of Mrs. Edmund N. Brown, who replaced Wilbur F. Chandler in February 1931. Madie Brown was a political activist, a leader in the women's club movement, and a longtime lobbyist for parks in the city of San Francisco where she had worked closely with James Rolph during his tenure as mayor. Her very active and strong personal interest in park matters made her another valuable addition to the commission.

In December 1932, after five full years on the commission, Burnham and O'Melveny resigned without fanfare and were quietly replaced by William T. Hart of Carlsbad, and P. E. Hatch of Long Beach. They took their park commission responsibilities seriously and the commission was able to continue its work with a minimum of disruption.

In November and December 1934, however, political circumstances surrounding the commission changed abruptly. Governor Rolph had died of a heart attack during the primary election campaign of June 1934. Thereafter, the Lieutenant Governor Frank F. Merriam had continued Rolph's more or less benevolent policy toward state parks. But in November, immediately after he was elected governor in his own right, Merriam began to remove

Zanetta House,
San Juan Bautista
State Historic Park.

and replace many top level administrators.

With no warning, and offering only the flimsiest of explanations, the governor ousted Colonel Wing, chief of the Division of Parks, Laura E. Gregory, secretary to the State Park Commission, and several other employees of the Division of Parks including Percy French, the highly respected superintendent of north coast redwood parks,

Castro House through
an archway of Mission
San Juan Bautista.

Harriet E. "Petey" Weaver, for many years a nature guide and recreation leader at Big Basin and Big Sur.

Roland A. Wilson, warden at Point Lobos from 1933 to 1954.

who had been closely associated with the Save-the-Redwoods League and with the north coast parks almost from their inception. All of these career employees were replaced by people recommended by the newly elected governor. Political patronage was surely not new to state government, but it had never before been a factor in the state park program.

The protest that ensued was loud and clear. Three members of the commission led the way by issuing a statement to the press in which they accused the governor of acting hastily and in bad faith. According to the statement, Wing, Gregory, and the others had all been doing excellent work. All had been "encouraged by the State Park Commission to take these positions on the assurance that they were non-political, and that their tenure would not be disturbed so long as they gave meritorius service." Colby explained that the statement was "given to the press with the firm conviction that the state parks are in a critical condition and need public support at this juncture." Introduction of the "spoils system" into state parks matters, Colby continued, threatened the continuation of federal participation in park development programs, and was bound to undermine public confidence and support. The new park system employees selected by the governor might be "estimable" and "nice enough" as individuals, but they were "persons who, for the most part, as far as any state park sympathies or previous park activities are concerned, are unqualified to hold the positions to which they have been appointed."

Newton Drury learned of the governor's actions late one night while traveling in the Central Valley on park

business. Immediately—disregarding the hour—he stopped and placed a telephone call to John C. Merriam in Washington, D.C. It was midnight in Tracy, California, and 3:00 a.m. in Washington, but Merriam accepted the call and after a brief discussion promised to do what he could first thing in the morning "to stop the havoc." A few hours later, true to his promise, he called Governor Merriam and discussed the park situation with him at length. The two men were first cousins and had known each other from childhood. As young men they had been in the habit of taking long walks through the fields of Iowa. The details of their long-distance conversation in December 1934 are not a matter of record, but shortly afterward Percy French was re-instated as superintendent of the north coast redwood parks, and no further upheavals took place among the ranks of State Park System employees.

The governor did not re-instate Colonel Wing or Mrs. Gregory, but both of these people were quickly hired by the federal government to help administer state park conservation work then being carried out by the CCC and other unemployment relief agencies. Gregory was put in charge of clerical services, and Colonel Wing became the official liaison officer between the Department of the Interior and the California State Park System.

The new chief of the California Division of Parks, James A. Snook, had no credentials and little or no interest in parks and outdoor recreation. Nor did he ever manage to gain the confidence of the commission during his time as

E. C. "Percy" French, superintendent of the Northern District from 1931 until his retirement in September 1953.

chief of the division. His administration was wracked by a stream of minor disputes and controversies that finally led the commission to demand his resignation in September 1936. To replace him, the commission created a three-man executive committee to administer the Division of Parks. This committee consisted of the chief (or acting chief) of the Division of Parks, the investigating officer, and the state park landscape engineer. Theoretically this meant that Newton Drury as investigating officer, Daniel Hull as landscape engineer, and J. H. Covington as secretary to the commission and acting chief of the division, were jointly responsible for interpreting and carrying out commission policy. As a practical reality, Drury did most of the thinking and wrote up most of the reports and recommendations for commission action. This arrangement continued even after April 1937, when Governor Merriam appointed a former Los Angeles City Council member, A. E. "Chick" Henning, to the position of chief. A businessman and San Pedro Chamber of Commerce leader, Henning had no practical park experience, and the executive committee was therefore helpful to him as he took up his new responsibilities.

The executive committee, and the extension of civil service protection to more state employees in 1936, tended to protect the park system from unfortunate partisan political interference. But the trend of events was nevertheless carrying the park system as a whole into ever deeper political waters.

In November 1936, the people of California were asked to vote on a proposal whereby several oil companies would pay royalties for the privilege of removing oil from state-owned tidelands or submerged lands along the

State Park Employees Conference at Big Basin in 1938. Left to right: Everett Powell, Bill Kenyon, Al Salzgeber, Clyde Newlin, Earl Hanson, Leo Frey. A committee was appointed to recommend a uniform for park system field employees.

California coastline. The campaign on behalf of the measure was conducted under the slogan "Save-Our-Beaches," and the State Park Commission endorsed the measure because it promised to provide millions of dollars for state park programs. This prospect was especially appealing to the commission because regular state funding for parks was painfully limited and yet groups and individuals in every part of the state were clamoring for more parks, more development of existing parks, and for state administration of park areas then being cared for by cities, counties, and other local agencies.

Opponents of the oil royalties measure charged that the proposed royalty rate of 14 2/7 percent amounted to a "giveaway." Moreover, they said, since competitive bidding would not be required under the law, just one company, Standard Oil, would reap almost the entire benefit.

The issue received a great deal of public attention because of the huge sums of money that were involved. The state-owned oil reserve just offshore from Huntington Beach, for example, was estimated to be worth $500 million dollars. The issue took on a highly partisan political flavor when it became apparent that the Republican governor, Frank F. Merriam, and his administration were in favor of the measure, whereas the Democrats and various small oil companies were rallying behind Senator Culbert Olson, chairman of a senate committee charged with investigating the whole question of oil and gas extraction from state lands.

The statewide ballot measure was defeated in November 1936, but the oil royalties issue continued to be highly controversial. It also continued to be intertwined with state park interests in terms of both funding and beach development for recreation, as opposed to oil and gas production purposes. Senator Olson continued to press his investigation and along the way, in November 1936, invited Will Colby and another commission member to explain the role of the State Park Commission in the recently concluded "Save-Our-Beaches" campaign. Colby testified fully and without reservation. He indicated that commission endorsement had not been based on the overall merits of the proposition, but simply on the fact that it would have provided badly needed funds for the park program.

Colby and the commission were not accused of any wrong-doing, and Colby's testimony further confirmed the general impression that the commission's action had been entirely honorable even if, in some eyes, it had seemed misguided.

In March 1938 Governor Merriam approved legislation that set up a State Lands Commission to administer state-owned oil and gas reserves. This new legislation also provided for competitive bidding, and required that 30 percent of all state income from oil royalties be deposited in a State Park Acquisition and Maintenance Fund. Later, when State Park System income from this source fell below expectations, the park fund share was increased to 70 percent. But even that step did not immediately provide all the park acquisition funds that were needed, because the legislature and the director of finance decided to "borrow" from the fund for other state purposes, and because—still later—the fund was "impounded" while several complicated legal issues were argued on the state, national, and international levels.

This linkage of relatively uncontroversial, non-partisan state park matters with highly controversial, highly partisan oil royalty matters, eventually led to a complete revision of state park policy-making procedures. Gradually, perhaps inevitably, the State Park Commission was stripped of its administrative responsibilities and cast in an advisory role. Meanwhile, the legislature, the governor and the governor's administrative appointees have come to play an ever larger role in park policy-making and park-funding decisions.

An early sample of what was to come occurred in November 1936 when Governor Merriam began to insist, rather than merely suggest, that Colby resign from the commission. Merriam's acceptance of Colby's resignation, effective November 21, 1936, marked the end of an era, for Colby was the last remaining member of the original commission, and had been chairman of the commission throughout its nine-year history.

Disheartened by Colby's departure and by what he felt was inappropriate partisan interference with park matters, Joseph R. Knowland considered resigning from the commission. But he finally decided, as he told Colby, "that it might be better to remain on for a while and see what may happen." In

Third annual State Park Employees Conference, Big Basin 1940. Kneeling at left front is Darwin Tate.

Borrego Palm Canyon, Anza Borrego Desert State Park. Below: *Borrego Valley.*

January 1937, at the first meeting after Colby's resignation, Knowland was elected chairman of the commission. He was still serving in that capacity two years later when Culbert Olson, shortly after his inauguration as governor, demanded that Knowland resign.

In July 1939, Governor Olson replaced all the other members of the commission as well, and beyond that announced the appointment of Darwin Tate as chief of the Division of Parks replacing Henning. Like Henning and Snook, his immediate predecessors, Tate had no practical experience in park matters. He did have a degree in horticulture, but his primary experience was in business and politics. Like Hen-

Torrey Pines State Reserve.

ning, he was a former member of the Los Angeles City Council. Impatient with protocol, he was happiest when he could get out to one of the parks and supervise the construction of some new recreational facility—a swimming pool, a ski-lift, a road, a restroom—whatever he felt would increase public enjoyment. His tendency to free-wheel, to ignore protocol, budget restraints, and even some long-established commission policies, brought him into repeated conflict with park enthusiasts including the Point Lobos Association, the Save-the-Redwoods League, and other early supporters of the State Park System.

The newly appointed State Park Commission members, on the other hand, were relatively unfamiliar with the parks and with established park policies. They were likely, therefore, to go along with some kinds of "improvement" proposals that more experience might have warned them against. Leading members of the staff sometimes found this situation hard to live with.

In August 1939 in a confidential memo to John C. Merriam, Drury de-

scribed some of his efforts to defend the State Park System. "I feel something like a duenna who has a beautiful young girl in charge and cannot nap for a moment. There are so many fool proposals being made for development, use and 'improvement' in the state parks that I have had to select for opposition those which were most crucial in order not to dissipate whatever influence I might have through degenerating into a chronic scold."

Still, amid all the trials and tribulations of this time, there were a few triumphs. Two magnificent redwood areas —the Mill Creek redwoods of Del Norte County, and the Avenue-of-the-Giants in Humboldt County—were acquired for park purposes, using a combination of oil royalties and matching contributions from the Save-the-Redwoods League. Because of the continuing shortage of state park acquisition funds, both of these areas were acquired under a lease-contract arrangement approved by the legislature in 1937. The new legislation made it possible for the state to pay for the land on an installment

basis parcel-by-parcel, year-by-year.

Little or no money was required to expand Anza-Borrego Desert State Park where thousands of acres of federal lands were still available to the State Park System at no cost other than the filing fees of one dollar per 80 acres. Money for this purpose had been pledged to the state by the Sierra Club and other conservation organizations, but park expansion was hotly opposed by San Diego County mining and grazing interests, who launched an all-out fight to block park expansion in favor of private use and development of the area. Hearings were held both by the State Park Commission and the Federal Lands Commission and finally, despite continued protest from a number of local interests, the park commission voted to proceed with expansion.

Public opinion on the general question of public preservation versus private exploitation of state park areas was tested in November 1940, when the people of California voted overwhelmingly—5½ to 1—against a proposal to sell off those parks or portions

Far left: *CCC camp at Palomar Mountain State Park.* Left: *CCC seasonal camp at D. L. Bliss State Park.*

of parks in which mining or grazing might be feasible.

On August 13, 1940 Newton Drury left state service in order to accept the position of director of the National Park Service. The position had also been offered to him in 1933, but he had elected then to stay in California and continue his work on behalf of the State Park System. In 1940, however, when Secretary of the Interior Harold L. Ickes once again offered him the job, he decided to accept. He had been recommended for the position by John C. Merriam and the National Parks Advisory Committee on the basis of his extraordinary accomplishments on behalf of both the Save-the-Redwoods League and the California State Park System. In its official letter of recommendation, the committee referred to Drury as unquestionably "the number one park man in America today."

Before his departure and in response to a State Park Commission request, Drury filed a detailed report on land acquisition matters in which he spelled

out a strategy whereby all of the most pressing acquisition problems could be solved through the use of oil royalty funds in combination with gifts from private or local government sources. In the months and years that followed Drury's departure, however, there were many setbacks. Income from oil royalties declined, matching funds became more difficult to obtain, and many acquisition proposals had to be rejected by the commission for lack of funds.

Despite the general slow-down in acquisition matters, however, the Save-the-Redwoods League managed to continue its fund-raising program, and with Aubrey Drury filling in for his brother Newton as secretary of the league, the state's redwood park acquisition program at Mill Creek and the Avenue-of-the-Giants continued on schedule. At the same time, mounting pressure from several south coast cities and counties led to the acquisition of a number of south coast beach areas including Will Rogers State Beach, and additions to Huntington and Doheny

State Beaches. These acquisitions were made possible by special legislation in 1941 that provided $600,000 for beach acquisition including $100,000 that could be spent by the state without matching funds. Because matching funds were not forthcoming, most of the remaining $500,000 was never spent.

In 1940 and 1941 the threat of war loomed ever larger on the horizon. War-related manufacturing began to take up the slack in employment, and the federal government closed out its unemployment relief programs—including the CCC and WPA—leaving a number of barracks and camp facilities standing empty in various state parks. Before long, U. S. military authorities approached Darwin Tate and the State Park Commission about the possibility of "temporary" military occupation of the old CCC camps and adjacent park areas. By April 1941 some 8,000 troops were using the state parks of California for housing, recreation, and training maneuvers. By the summer of 1941 the

La Purisima Mission State Historic Park. Facing page: *Interior of the church. Reconstruction by the CCC; color and trim restoration by the WPA.* Below: *The restored bell tower.*

number of troops in park areas had risen to 20,000.

At about this time the magnificent reconstruction and restoration work that the CCC had been doing at La Purisima Mission State Historic Park since 1934, was finally completed. To celebrate this accomplishment, a dedication ceremony was arranged for the fateful weekend of December 6 and 7, 1941.

Thereafter, following the official declaration of war by FDR on December 8, 1941, military use of state park areas became even more intense. Silver Strand was completely taken over by the U. S. Navy and used for many things including—as of about 1943— amphibious landing practice.

Calaveras Big Trees State Park was used to house Army Air Corps trainees from various training centers in the Central Valley. The CCC barracks at Pfeiffer Big Sur housed a coastal patrol unit, and both Big Basin and Big Sur State Parks were used for training maneuvers by troops stationed at Fort Ord. Mount Tamalpais State Park was closed to the public. The beacon atop Mount Diablo was shut down for the duration. The House of Gold in Monterey was used as a Red Cross headquarters. Along the coast, various park units were entirely closed to the public. Patrick's Point was given over to a number of machine gun emplacements. Point Lobos served as a high security military observation station, and no one —not even the park warden—was allowed to enter the area.

Park visitation decreased sharply during the next three years as a result of many factors including the shortage of gasoline and tires. Anza-Borrego Desert State Park was closed for the duration, and the resident ranger assigned elsewhere. Gas and tire rationing also made it difficult to patrol the more widely scattered parks, and a critical shortage of state park personnel developed in 1942 as more and more park system employees joined the armed services or took more highly paid defense work. As a result of these wartime factors, the California State Park System staggered on the verge of complete obscurity.

Lake Tahoe shoreline from Rubicon Point, D. L. Bliss State Park.

7 The Postwar Years

"The heart of our movement [the park movement] is a thing of the spirit, although the material we deal with is land. It is a high calling that has as its purpose to assure the people of the future that they will have the great experiences in the out-of-doors that we have had. In the midst of the turmoil of administration and the perfection of our techniques we must remember this."

Newton B. Drury, 1957

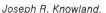
Joseph R. Knowland.

Postwar Tourism and Recreation Demand

Public interest in the California State Park System revived quickly after the conclusion of World War II. Because gas rationing and other wartime restraints had put a sharp limit on tourism, many a dream about the postwar era involved travel plans. Throughout the war, moreover, most people had worked long hours six and seven days a week, and thereby accumulated sizeable cash reserves as well as tremendous amounts of unused vacation time. Many defense workers had arrived in California after the war was already underway and had never been able to get out and see very much of the world famous California landscape. Others, including many native Californians, found themselves living in urban areas for the first time—often in severely overcrowded, temporary, wartime housing. They and the war veterans who began to return to their homes in 1945 were eager to revisit their favorite prewar haunts, including many of the state beaches and parks. On top of all this, the general postwar shift to a five-day work week meant that, quite suddenly, there was more leisure time available for travel than ever before.

Fortunately, the governor, the legislature, the State Park Commission, and State Park System staff members had had foresight enough to predict and prepare to meet postwar park and recreation needs. Preparations had begun as early as 1943 when the legislature provided funding for plans, surveys, and other preliminary steps leading to the inauguration of a bold and visionary postwar state park program.

The development of such a program was a matter of direct personal interest to Earl Warren, who had replaced Culbert Olson as governor in January 1943. Warren had run a "non-partisan" or "bi-partisan" campaign and had received significant support from both Republicans and Democrats. His appointments, including those to the State Park Commission, reflected his non-partisan approach. Isadore Dockweiler was asked to continue on the commission even though he was an Olson appointee and a longtime Democrat closely associated with FDR. Further defying partisan political traditions,

Warren also appointed another leading Democrat, his close friend Leo Carrillo, the popular entertainer and Hollywood personality. Carrillo had played an extremely important role in Warren's gubernatorial campaign as leader of the "Loyal Democrats, Warren for Governor Committee." Of course, Carrillo was not only a famous personality and a Democrat. He was a native Californian and an enthusiastic student of Californiana whose family had been in the state for many generations.

Governor Warren also appointed George Waldner, editor and publisher of the *Ferndale Enterprise,* and Alfred Harrell, editor and publisher of the *Bakersfield Californian.* But the appointment that must have pleased the governor most of all was that of his longtime political mentor and publisher of the *Oakland Tribune,* Joseph R. Knowland, whose commitment to historical preservation and other state park matters was by that time a matter of legend.

The State Park Commission appointed by Governor Warren immediately selected Knowland as its chairman, and soon afterward brought in A. E. "Chick" Henning as chief of the division. Henning had experience in the job, having served as chief from April 1937 to July 1939. He was also considered an excellent administrator who knew how to promote efficiency through a sense of team spirit.

The new commission quickly began to assert itself and to restore that extraordinary sense of idealism which had characterized the very earliest years of the park system's existence. The tree-cutting policy of the previous administration was investigated and a new policy clearly delineated so that no further tree cutting would occur without apparent benefit to the park system. War Department requests for the use of park areas were no longer granted automatically. Instead, they were carefully screened to determine the probable impact of the proposed use and the degree of real need. If suitable alternative sites were available outside park boundaries, military authorities were encouraged to go elsewhere and allow the parks to be preserved for park purposes.

In May 1944, the commission was still further strengthened when the gov-

The executive staff about 1948.
Left to right: A. E. Henning, Dan Hull, J. H. Covington, Ernest B. Camper.

ernor appointed Charles Kasch of Ukiah to replace Waldner, who had been called away to active duty with the armed forces. Kasch and Warren had been close friends ever since their student days at the University of California. But Kasch was also a very dedicated friend of the park movement. He objected forthrightly and persuasively to commercial exploitation of park areas simply for the purpose of generating revenue. He argued that the commission was not legally authorized to permit use of the parks in any way that did not clearly further the purposes for which they had been created. Following his lead, the commission refused to grant any more permits for commercial radio antennas on the upper slopes of Mount Diablo. They also refused to renew grazing permits at Palomar Mountain State Park, and even went so far as to object to the proposal then being put forward by various Palm Springs businessmen that a tram be constructed up the precipitous eastern face of Mount San Jacinto.

The peak and upper portions of Mount San Jacinto had been set aside in order to preserve their wilderness qualities, Kasch argued. The tram, tram station, hotel, ski-runs, and associated tourist facilities then being proposed were therefore in direct conflict with established State Park Commission policy. It soon became apparent, however, that this issue could not be easily resolved, for the tram concept had strong political support. The result was a continuing and at times bitter debate that eventually took on statewide and even national significance as an example—a symbol—of the conflict between wilderness and developmental values.

Governor Warren unveiled his "Postwar Reconstruction and Redevelopment Program" in January 1945. The $60 million state surplus inherited from the Olson administration had been deliberately augmented year by year, so that by the end of the war Warren had some $300 million on hand with which to ease the transition from an emergency wartime economy to a stable peacetime economy. In the field of

parks and recreation the governor called for support of an "Omnibus Park Acquisition Bill" that would provide $10 million for beach acquisition and $5 million for inland park acquisition. The two-to-one emphasis on beach acquisition was a response to the pressure that had been building up even before the war for a more ambitious, fast-moving, beach acquisition program, especially in southern California. Pressure of this same kind had already resulted in a name change for the Division of Parks; as of 1941, it had become the Division of Beaches and Parks. Going still further in 1943, the legislature had abolished the "State Park Maintenance and Acquisition Fund" and created two new funds, the "State Park Fund" and the "State Beach Fund," a step that made it possible to keep beach acquisition funds separate from other park acquisition or maintenance funds.

The 1945 Omnibus Acquisition Bill also stressed the importance of providing recreational facilities "for those sections of the state where such facilities are not now available and particularly in the valley, desert, and mountain areas of the interior." Governor Warren's continuing concern about the postwar need for new recreational programs and facilities was also apparent in the 1947 legislation that created a Recreation Commission and director of recreation completely separate from the Division of Beaches and Parks. This new agency was intended to provide leadership and coordinate state support for city, county, and other local park and recreation agencies.

Along with the $15 million Omnibus Park Acquisition Bill, a number of other park-related bills also sailed through the legislature in 1945. One of them provided funds for planning a statewide system of riding and hiking trails. Other bills designated specific beach and park acquisitions and authorized increases in staff to handle acquisition, development, and other aspects of park system expansion. The legislature also approved AB2075, providing for staggered four-year terms of office for State Park Commission members. The measure was intended to provide a small but significant buffer between the commission and the "pleasure of the governor." Similar legislation had been passed only to be vetoed on several

previous occasions, but in 1945 Governor Warren signed the measure along with what some observers called an "avalanche" of park-related legislation. Altogether, as A. E. Henning pointed out, this legislation amounted to "the largest expansion and development program in the history of the State Park System."

While all this legislative activity was underway in Sacramento during the spring and early summer of 1945, the world was witness to an extraordinary succession of momentous events: President Roosevelt died in April; the United Nations held its first formal meetings in San Francisco in May; Victory in Europe—V.E. Day—was celebrated that same month, and meanwhile the Battle of Okinawa, as well as other military events, made it ever more obvious that the war with Japan was coming to an end.

No one was prepared, however, for the war to end as suddenly as it did in August 1945 after the bombing of Hiroshima and Nagasaki. In the days and weeks that followed, American military veterans began to stream in from the Pacific War Zone, and joyous celebrations were held everywhere in California and across the nation to mark not only the end of the war and the reunion of families, but also the end of wartime restraints of all kinds.

Unprecedented numbers of people took to the road—and to the parks. The steep, winding road through Mount Tamalpais State Park, for example, had never seen more than 120 cars in a single day. But on the first weekend after the end of gas rationing, a traffic count revealed that more than 220 cars were using the road *per hour!* Visitors to the Founders' Tree in Humboldt Redwoods State Park increased from an average of 50 per day to 500 per day. Campgrounds in the redwood parks overflowed, and people took refuge alongside the highway wherever they could. Restaurants and other park concession operators ran out of supplies and had to close down. Doheny State Beach was overwhelmed with visitors, especially on the weekends when the park staff was forced to work virtually around the clock. One tired ranger described the situation in a note to headquarters that concluded, "If we hold out until after Labor Day we will be okay."

Waiting for camp space; first come, first served. Entrance to D. L. Bliss State Park about 1950.

Growing Pains

Gearing up to meet the postwar boom in park and recreation demand was a complex and difficult process for it involved extensive planning and coordination between state and local governments. This coordinated planning was specifically mandated by the Omnibus Park Bill of 1945, which required each county to develop a masterplan for beach and park acquisition. The State Park Commission was to coordinate these plans into one statewide masterplan, and set priorities for action by the Division of Beaches and Parks. In the immediate aftermath of World War II, however, the Division of Beaches and Parks and many cities and counties were understaffed, especially in terms of the kind of technical capability needed to compile detailed engineering and appraisal information. Before such problems could be solved, governmental budgets had to be revised and that, of course, involved a welter of interrelated political factors.

In the general euphoria that followed the conclusion of World War II, however, problems of every kind were overcome with dispatch. War veterans streaming back to civilian life were eager for meaningful peacetime work. Along with other corporations and public agencies, the Division of Beaches and Parks gave its returning war veterans a warm welcome, put them back to work, promoted them, and began to add large numbers of new employees. Parks that had been closed for the duration of the war were reopened, and others—some of them never before open to the public due to a general shortage of field personnel—were staffed for the first time. The headquarters staff, which had been moved to Sacramento in 1941 by the Olson administration, was increased from five to 30 people and then reorganized into five sections. Most of these new headquarters people were engineers, planners, or other specialists needed to cope with the problems of postwar expansion and development.

Colonel Edwin C. Kelton was hired in June 1945 to supervise planning and development of shoreline areas. Kelton brought impressive credentials to his work on behalf of the Division of Beaches and Parks. After serving in the U.S. Army Corps of Engineers during World War I he had gone on to supervise major construction programs for public agencies around the world. A man of boundless energy and quiet but contagious enthusiasm, he managed to coordinate the whole postwar shoreline masterplanning effort, and then went on to supervise planning, engineering, and actual development of shoreline and other park areas. By the time he decided to retire in 1952, 24 new beaches and parks had been acquired, and almost $10 million worth of state park development projects had been completed. Construction activity under Colonel Kelton's direction reached a peak in 1949 when the value of work put in place reached $500,000 per month. (It should be remembered, of course, that throughout the 1950s and '60s, the California Division of Highways was spending a million dollars a day and more.)

In December 1945, the State Park Commission once again hired Frederick Law Olmsted as an advisor on inland park acquisition and development. Olmsted was already working closely with the Save-the-Redwoods League on two state park matters: acquisition of the Calaveras South Grove, and highway design in several north coast redwood parks. The commission now asked him to give special attention to the expansion and development of Columbia State Historic Monument, and to the feasibility of scenic parkways along the Sacramento and San Joaquin Rivers. He was also asked to review the whole question of how best to round out the park system. Many of Olmsted's 1928 recommendations had been followed by this time, but the matching provision had made it difficult or impossible for the state to acquire parks in certain valley, desert, and mountain areas of the interior.

Olmsted set to work on these questions immediately, and, although he did not file a final report until 1950, he did submit progress reports to the commission from time to time. Olmsted's influence quickly became pervasive. His reports and recommendations were greatly respected, almost universally accepted, and seldom ignored. Quoted, paraphrased, expanded, or perhaps revised somewhat, his language and ideas tended to form the backbone of countless official reports and memorandums.

In August 1943, in order to improve communication and morale within the Division of Beaches and Parks, A. E. Henning had started publishing a simple little "house organ." Henning himself edited the first issue, which ran nine mimeographed pages and included current news items, biographical profiles of commission members, and the names and addresses of all seventy-three field employees. Henning also asked the employees of the division if they were interested in having such a publication as a regular feature. Would they send in the necessary information to make it worthwhile? Would they share the editorial work—rotating the editorship from issue to issue?

District Superintendents Conference, December 1949. Front row, left to right: Ronald E. Miller, John Hennessey, J. H. Covington, A. E. Henning, Earl Hanson, Col. E. C. Kelton. Standing, left to right: Robert Coon, Murrell Gregory, Ernest B. Camper, George Holmboe, Everett Powell, Llewellyn Griffith, Percy French, Jess Chaffee, Gene Velzy, Lee Blaisdell, Jack Knight, Bill Kenyon, Clyde Newlin.

The response was overwhelmingly favorable, and subsequent editions began to appear in October 1943. Names were suggested: ''Bear Facts,'' ''Grizzly Grist,'' ''Park Views and News,'' ''The Voice of the Beaches and Parks,'' ''Park Trailer and Raft,'' ''Nuggets and Foam,'' ''Speeches and Barks.'' Both field and headquarters personnel took turns editing the little newsletter, and a spirit of

Calaveras Big Trees State Park. Above: The Stanislaus River. *Right: Giant Sequoias.*

The Mendocino coastline, Salt Point State Park.

friendly competition soon began to make it bigger and better.

First permanent editor of the publication was Edward F. Dolder, who had worked before the war as a newspaperman and then as a public information officer for the California Department of Natural Resources. Dolder joined the Division of Beaches and Parks in February 1946 as supervisor of conservation education. This newly created position was intended to be a step toward upgrading the division's education and interpretive programs. Dolder was to hire and train new interpretive personnel ("nature guides" and "recreation leaders"). He was to write and supervise the publication of park fold-

ers, take photographs, prepare slide programs, acquire projectors and other equipment for field interpretation programs.

That first season Dolder logged 9,500 miles of travel as he familiarized himself with the parks, park personnel, and current interpretive programs. He took hundreds of photographs for use in slide programs and publicity files. He also conferred with field personnel and others about how to formalize, promote, and develop a coherent statewide public information and interpretive program. The Division of Beaches and Parks was preparing to play a more active role in the field of environmental education.

The Postwar Land Acquisition Program

A Land Section was established within the Division of Beaches and Parks in 1946 in order to expedite land acquisition matters. As state government expanded during the post war years, official procedures became more complex. And as funds from the Omnibus Park Bill of 1945 enabled the park system to begin acquiring land once again, the usual array of appraisals, offers, counter-offers, easements, conditions, and other individual agreements had to be drawn up on literally hundreds of parcels of land in virtually every corner

81

Mr. & Mrs. Frederick Law Olmsted at Prairie Creek Redwoods State Park, July 1953.

Edward F. Dolder.

of the state. Acquisition priorities, moreover, had to be coordinated with the availability of local matching funds, which were required by the 1945 legislation just as they had been under the original state park legislation. To supervise this increasingly complex process the Division hired John A. Hennessey, a professional real estate appraiser with twenty years of experience with the Los Angeles Department of Water and Power.

The first state park to be acquired under the provisions of the Omnibus Park Bill of 1945 was Samuel P. Taylor State Park in Marin County. The heart of the project, Camp Taylor, was a beautiful redwood-filled canyon area that had become popular as early as 1878 as a privately owned resort and campground. Matching funds for this project were provided by the Tamalpais Conservation Club, the Marin Nature Group, and other conservation-minded people in Marin County.

Other groups, particularly the Save-the-Redwoods League, provided funds or gifts of land for matching purposes on behalf of other park projects throughout the postwar years. But more often it was a city or county or other public agency that provided the necessary matching value. The first state beach to be acquired after the war, for example, was San Buenaventura State Beach in Ventura County. In this case, soon after the county master-plan was completed, the City of Ventura turned over to the state by gift deed some 2,000 feet of beach frontage and a 1,900-foot-long fishing pier complete with concession operation—in all, a gift valued at nearly a half-million dollars. This gift constituted matching value and enabled the state to expend an equal amount of beach acquisition funds at San Buenaventura and elsewhere along the coast.

Other beaches and parks acquired during this same period—all on the basis of matching funds—included Donner Memorial State Park at Donner Lake in the Sierra Nevada, Portola Redwoods State Park in San Mateo County, Robert Louis Stevenson State Park high

atop Mount Saint Helena in Napa County, the Los Angeles State and County Arboretum in Los Angeles, Knowland State Arboretum and Park in Oakland, and Montgomery Woods State Park in Mendocino County. Along with the acquisition of these new park units, there were major additions to Humboldt Redwoods, Prairie Creek Redwoods, and Jedediah Smith Redwoods State Parks in the north coast region and to Columbia State Historic Park in Tuolumne County. Important beach acquisitions included Cardiff, La Costa, Moonlight, and Ponto State Beaches in San Diego County, Corona Del Mar State Beach in Orange County, and Dockweiler State Beach in Los Angeles County (named in honor of State Park Commissioner Isadore Dockweiler after his death in 1947). By far the most ambitious beach acquisition from a financial point of view was Santa Monica State beach in Los Angeles County, where in 1948 the state invested $4.4 million in state beach acquisition funds in order to acquire 9,833 feet of ocean frontage. In central and northern California the state acquired Capitola and Manresa State Beaches in Santa Cruz County, Stinson Beach and Tomales Bay State Parks in Marin County, and MacKerricher State Beach in Mendocino County.

Despite rapid growth, however, the State Park System could not keep up with public demand for still more and better park and recreation opportunities. Most parks and beaches were overcrowded during prime vacation periods. Waiting lines were common at many park entrance stations and uncounted numbers of people had to be turned away. The trouble was that Cali-

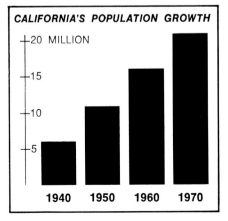

CALIFORNIA'S POPULATION GROWTH

20 MILLION

15

10

5

| 1940 | 1950 | 1960 | 1970 |

fornia had become a "hotspot." Tourists from all over the nation were flocking to the state on a seasonal basis, and literally hundreds of thousands of people were migrating to California, entering the workforce and taking up permanent residence. Total population of the state increased by one million in the two years following the war, and by nearly four million between 1940 and 1950. Moreover, despite all the pressures of very rapid growth and the problems associated with transition to a peacetime economy, California remained relatively prosperous so that Californians as a whole enjoyed both high income (25 percent above the national average) and abundant leisure. Still, the park system would have come far closer to meeting the skyrocketing park and recreation demand if oil royalty funds had continued to be available for the acquisition and development of new parks. But in June 1947, as a result of a U.S. Supreme Court ruling, the flow of oil royalties suddenly stopped.

Legislative and congressional debate over the ownership of tideland and offshore oil reserves had been proceeding for years, but in 1945, in an effort to resolve the issue once and for all, U.S. Attorney General Francis Biddle filed suit in Los Angeles District Court in the first great legal move by the federal government to take over the submerged lands. The matter went to the U.S. Supreme Court which decided in favor of the federal government. The question then arose, however, as to just where the boundary should be drawn between state and federal jurisdiction of submerged lands. To resolve this issue, a "special master in chancery" was appointed to study the problem and make a recommendation. Until the boundary could be determined, the Supreme Court ruled, all oil royalty revenues were to be impounded.

State Park System supporters, including many state legislators and other state and local interests, were outraged. The Supreme Court ruling was improper, they said. It overturned 150 years of precedent. State Senator

Marshall Gold Discovery State Historic Park. In January 1948 an estimated 75,000 people attended the California Gold Discovery Centennial Celebration at Coloma. Speakers' stand, right to left: State Park Commissioners J. R. Knowland, Leo Carrillo, Charles Kasch; Governor Earl Warren.

State Park Commission meeting informally in the home of Leo Carrillo, February 1947. Carrillo at left with hand on child's shoulder.

Arthur H. Breed, a longtime friend of the park system and chairman of the State Joint Interim Committee on Tidelands, issued a statement to the press in which he said: "This impoundment, and the possible full loss of all income for the State Park System, jeopardizes the recreational activities of every man, woman, and child in the state. This is a problem which affects all plans to acquire new beaches and parks . . . and thus its effect reaches down into the smallest communities of the state, particularly along the coast."

Senator Breed also explained that he and other political leaders were working closely with U.S. Senator William F. Knowland, who had already introduced congressional legislation designed to return ownership of offshore oil reserves to the State of California. Knowland had been appointed to the U.S. Senate in 1945 by Governor Warren after the mid-term retirement of Hiram Johnson. He was the son of State Park Commission Chairman Joseph R. Knowland, and was therefore quite familiar with the state park program in California. Despite this great flurry of political excitement, however, no imme-

diate resolution of the problem was possible, and as weeks of delay turned into months and years, millions of dollars of impounded oil royalty funds began to accumulate—and the State Park System found itself increasingly unable to carry out its expansion program.

The Return of Newton Drury

When Newton Drury left California in August 1940 to assume his responsibilities in Washington, D.C. as director of the National Park Service, he intended to stay for no more than a year or two before returning to California and to his position as secretary of the Save-the-Redwoods League. Once on the job in the nation's capital, however, he was so fascinated by the challenge that presented itself that he stayed on for more than a decade. During that time he was widely admired for his carefully reasoned, courageous, and eloquent defense of national park values, which were constantly being threatened by development proposals in the name of "the national emergency." After the war Drury led the movement to expand and

Newton B. Drury, 1951.

otherwise improve the national parks, and his accomplishments in this regard were also widely admired.

In 1951, at the time of his retirement from federal service, virtually every important conservation organization in the nation joined in a great celebration of Drury's many accomplishments. Their jointly sponsored testimonial statement concluded:

"We feel that our confidence in you when you entered upon your duties, and our high hopes for your administration have been justified, completely and abundantly. You have been the chief custodian of our country's greatest treasures, unique and irreplaceable, the superlative works of nature upon our land and the monuments of the history of our people. You have guarded these treasures with devotion and with courage as a sacred trust on behalf of countless generations to come, and you have known how to draw from them inspiration for the generation of the present. You have held high the ideals of a branch of the public service which has been notable for its ideals and its loyalty to them, and you have maintained and enhanced its great tradition."

Expedition to the South Grove, Calaveras Big Trees State Park, 1947, led by Sacramento businessman, philanthropist, and conservationist C. M. Goethe, at center.

The restored Mission San Francisco Solano de Sonoma, Sonoma State Historic Park. Below: Vallejo Home, Sonoma State Historic Park.

Statements of admiration and respect for Drury and his accomplishments were read into the Congressional Record in 1951 and also appeared in many newspapers and other journals of the time. Fanfare surrounding his departure from Washington, however, was soon followed by still more public notice, for shortly after his return to California he was appointed by Governor Earl Warren to serve as chief of the California Division of Beaches and Parks.

Drury and Warren had known each other since their undergraduate days at the University of California in Berkeley. Drury was also well known by Joseph R. Knowland and other members of the State Park Commission. And he was intimately acquainted with most of the state parks and many park system employees. He made an all-out effort, nevertheless, to visit the parks and renew his acquaintanceship with the places themselves and the people who cared most about them.

The preservation of natural phenomena was still his main interest. Development of the parks could come later, he

reasoned, but if people were interested in preserving the unique charm and attractiveness of the native landscape, they could not afford to delay further acquisition of land for park purposes. Beach acquisition was also a high priority of the Drury administration for, as he pointed out, only 75 miles of the 1,100-mile-long California coastline were publicly owned and accessible.

Drury also called for a stronger program of historical preservation and persuaded the legislature and the governor to appoint an Historical Landmarks Advisory Committee, as well as a full-time professional chief historian who could give "leadership, help, and inspiration to the fine corps of curators and rangers who are doing such an excellent job, now pretty much on their own, in protecting, maintaining, restoring and interpreting various eloquent reminders of California's colorful past." In January 1953, he persuaded Dr. V. Aubrey Neasham to leave his position as regional historian for the National Park Service and return to state service. An ideal candidate for the state position, Neasham was a dedicated student of California and western regional history. He was familiar with the State Park System through his consulting work for

The ruins of Wolf House, Jack London State Historic Park.

for the commission; and he had administered the state park-related historical research program sponsored by the W.P.A. during the 1930s.

Drury also did what he could to improve the capability of the Division of Beaches and Parks in terms of planning, landscape architecture, and engineering. The division already had competent people in each of these areas, but was far too thinly staffed to cope with a major expansion program. Drury wanted the division to have a team of experts who could go out into the field, become intimately familiar with each park, and draw up master-

plans one by one. These masterplans were intended to help the division avoid unwise development while providing the best possible facilities for park visitors. According to Drury, the hallmark of good park planning and development was *restraint*.

A natural landscape, he would point out, was likely to represent the interrelated operation of countless natural factors over centuries of time. And, by the same token, historic sites, settings, and artifacts were literally priceless and irreplaceable resources. Such things could be badly damaged or destroyed in a single afternoon by one misdirected

bulldozer, or one careless park planner. Those who were impatient for immediate and more extensive development of the parks were asked to think not only of themselves and the pressures of the moment, but also of past and future generations. As Drury succinctly phrased it, "People have a right to *use* the parks, of course. But no one generation has a right to *use them up.*"

With his special personal skills, Drury was able to solve many problems quickly, simply, and with a minimum of political conflict. Some situations, however, were too complicated and too pressurized to be resolved without con-

District Superintendents Conference about 1957. Standing left to right: *Gordon Kishbaugh, Jack Knight, Bill Kenyon, Newton Drury, Earl Hanson, Jess Chaffee, Jim Warren, Clyde Newlin.* Kneeling, left to right: *Elmer Aldrich, Harry Beddig, Ronald Miller, L. D. "Butch" Ewen, Everett Powell, Steve Wardwell, Fred Meyer.*

troversy. One such issue was the proposal to widen a portion of the "Redwood Highway" (U.S. 101 in northern California) into a four-lane, high-speed freeway that would run right through the heart of Humboldt Redwoods State Park. The issue had been simmering since the 1930s, but the postwar highway and housing construction boom, plus the development of bigger, better, faster logging and lumber trucks, brought the issue to a head in the late 1940s and early 1950s. The conflict was finally resolved in 1956 by a compromise proposal to move the highway to a less destructive route outside the principal redwood groves using $2.5 million of State Park System funds to help pay for the higher cost of construction on the new alignment.

Drury and leading conservationists from many parts of the nation believed that the highway should have been moved all the way outside the park rather than passing through any part of it. In their eyes the compromise route was still far too close to the major groves, and would do serious damage to park values near Dyerville where the new highway was to cross the South Fork of the Eel River. Nevertheless, all parties agreed that the final compromise arrangement was the best that could be achieved under the circumstances. At least the old, two-lane highway could now be used exclusively as a park road, and therefore remain a narrow, winding, scenic highway—one of the most spectacular in the world.

Another highway construction project that was hotly debated during the 1950s would have had disastrous consequences for D. L. Bliss and Emerald Bay State Parks at Lake Tahoe. The proposal was to bridge the entrance of Emerald Bay and build several miles of approach road that would, as Drury put it, "mutilate one of the great scenic areas of America and bisect two important state park camping areas." Fortunately for the park system and the people of California, this project was stopped in the state legislature when it became apparent that there was widespread and influential opposition to such a highway.

Drury and his administration also had to fight other threats to the State Park System including the proposed tramway and resort development at

Mount San Jacinto, logging of the still privately owned Calaveras South Grove, disruption of public use at Huntington Beach by construction of a proposed public utility plant, grazing within Anza-Borrego and other desert areas remarkable for their native flora. But throughout these and other difficulties, Drury remained unswervingly polite—firm, but always calm.

He looked upon the extremely rapid growth and development of California as a threat not only to the park system but to the beauty, livability, and economic well-being of the state. But he did not like to be always on the defensive. "As they say in the advertising business, we must have 'reason why copy' to explain nature conservation policies, and to prove the worth of our program as an essential part of our culture, as a gauge of our national dignity, as an assurance of national health and even of national sanity. This message needs to be expounded simply but dramatically, not just to the enthusiasts . . . but also to the layman and the legislator, to the man of affairs and the man in the street. This is not easy to do. It requires all the techniques of salesmanship and all the skills of propaganda, as practiced in commerce and

in civic affairs. But it must be done. The forces that are impinging on natural areas are doing it. And as Martin Luther said, 'There is no reason why the devil should have all the good tunes.' "

Drury believed that much of this job would have to be done by citizen groups that could operate freely outside the normal protocol and restraints of officialdom. Nevertheless, the Division of Beaches and Parks did have a right and even a responsibility to "explain its operations and its purposes to the people." Accordingly, Drury did what he could to improve the division's public information and interpretive programs. The number of seasonal naturalists, and the number of parks and historical sites featuring interpretive programs was increased year by year. Considerable attention was given to recruiting the best available people and giving them sufficient training to enable them to intelligently represent the park system at campfire programs and on guided walks and other interpretive activities. Each year, just prior to the peak travel season, a Naturalists' Training Conference was held. Drury always made it a point to participate. These conferences were set up and admin-

The new highway bridge across the South Fork of the Eel River, Humboldt Redwoods State Park.

Retouched aerial photo showing the route of the Emerald Bay bridge and highway as proposed during the 1950s.

U.S. 101 approaching Prairie Creek Redwoods State Park.

istered by Elmer Aldrich, who had replaced Ed Dolder as supervisor of conservation education in April 1949.

Drury held special meetings with interpretive personnel, wrote letters of commendation, spoke at various gatherings dealing with interpretive matters, and in one way or another managed to inspire enormous zeal, bringing people together in an almost religious sense, so that in many cases obstacles were overcome simply because people were confident that they were participating in an important program of uniquely enlightened and noble intent. Despite everyone's best efforts, however, budgetary support for the interpretive program remained meager, and a great deal had to be done on the basis of individual initiative and ingenuity, long hours of unpaid overtime, and gifts of artifacts, money, and other support from private sources.

The Drury years (1951-59) were also a time of great accomplishment in terms of park acquisition. Even prior to September 1954, while California's oil royalty funds were still impounded, Drury and various friends of the park movement found ways to get things done. Matching funds, as required under the Omnibus Park Bill of 1945, were provided by cities, counties, and private sources for beach and park areas such as Pueblo de Los Angeles (including Olverra Street) and Leo Carrillo State Beach in Los Angeles, Caswell Memorial State Park and George J. Hatfield State Recreation Area in the Central Valley, Carmel River State Beach and El Capitan State Beach on the coastline, and Emerald Bay State Park at Lake Tahoe.

Perhaps the most notable of these matching-fund efforts was the acquisition of the South Grove at Calaveras Big Trees. Announcement of the $2.8 million addition to Calaveras Big Trees State Park in April 1954 marked the culmination of a campaign that had begun before the turn of the century when both the north and south groves were

sold to a lumber company. During the 1940s and '50s, widespread and enthusiastic support for acquisition of the South Grove had been rekindled by the spirited campaign of the Calaveras Grove Association led by Adrienne Bradley and Stuart Gibbons. Major financial contributions to the campaign —including one million dollars from John D. Rockefeller, Jr.—were provided by the Save-the-Redwoods League.

Some park areas were acquired during these years at no cost to the state. Acquisition of Angel Island began in 1954 when the federal government turned over free of charge some 36 acres surrounding Hospital Cove. This and later additions to the island park in San Francisco Bay were brought about by the dedicated efforts of Caroline S. Livermore, Charles S. Winslow, and other members of the Marin Conservation League.

Henry Cowell Redwoods State Park was gift-deeded to the state in 1953 by the county of Santa Cruz (120 acres) and by Samuel H. Cowell (1,615 acres) in honor of his father, Henry Cowell. The area is made up of scenic canyon land and redwood forest on the San Lorenzo River near Felton, California. It includes the old Felton (or Welch) Grove in which Andrew Hill and Joseph Welch confronted each other in 1900. That confrontation, it will be remembered, was the incident that led to the creation of the Sempervirens Club and the subsequent acquisition of California Redwood Park in Big Basin.

During the Drury years other generous gifts to the State Park System by private parties included historic Pacific House, the Larkin House, and the Soberanes and Gutierrez Adobes in Monterey. Perhaps the most spectacular private gift of all, however, was that of the fabulous Hearst Castle at San Simeon. Negotiations leading to this extraordinary gift to the people of California began in 1951 shortly after the death of William Randolph Hearst, but legal complications led to lengthy delays in

the actual transfer of title. Finally, in June 1958, the castle and its immediate setting, *La Cuesta Encantada,* "The Enchanted Hill," were successfully opened to the visiting public. Since that time some eleven million people have toured this unique historic site.

Oil Royalties — Again!

In September 1954, following a number of national and even international legal decisions, California regained control of its offshore oil royalty funds. Impounded and accumulating since June 1947, the total amount theoretically earmarked for the Division of Beaches and Parks had climbed to some $31.6 million. Now, with that much money suddenly available and more still due to come in each year, many people, including many members of the state legislature, were eager to start spending. As early as 1952, anticipating this great rush of excitement, Drury had caused a five-year masterplan to be drawn up. Revised and updated each year thereafter, the plan was based in large part on the Olmsted reports of 1928 and 1950. It was intended to express the best possible professional judgment about the need for beaches and parks in various parts of the state, and the relative priority that should be given to individual projects in order to maintain a balanced statewide program. In the legislative rush, however, much of this careful planning was replaced by political considerations of every imaginable kind.

In their enthusiasm, the legislators put together a $15,932,500 Omnibus Park Bill, and then added another $3.5 million worth of individual park and beach acquisition appropriations. They called for abandonment of the matching principle that had been an integral part of both the 1928 bond act and the 1945 legislative act providing for park acquisition. And they called for the inauguration of a statewide program of roadside rests to be administered by

Bodie State Historic Park.

Shasta State Historic Park.

the Division of Beaches and Parks—a program the Division of Highways did not want to handle.

On July 9, 1955, Governor Goodwin Knight vetoed both the Omnibus Park Bill and the other separate bills for beach and park projects, and issued an explanatory statement to the public:

"I believe it is premature to appropriate large amounts of money for a major beach and park acquisition program before certain important policy questions have been clarified by legislation." Abandonment of the matching principle, he said, deserved far more careful consideration by the legislature. "The development of our Beach and Park System must be in accordance with a sound, prudent, comprehensive masterplan. Allocation of funds for this purpose should be through the regular budget process in accordance with a system of priorities as is done in other capital outlay budgeting and should not be on a basis of competition among members of the legislature through special bills."

In accordance with the governor's wishes, the State Park Commission held public hearings in both northern and southern California. Then on the basis of all available information, the staff of the division compiled a new five-year masterplan to cover the years 1956-61. The result was a 100-page report covering acquisition, development, maintenance and operating costs, as well as a number of special projects such as roadside rests, riding and hiking trails, etc. The report was published March 1, 1956, and submitted to the legislature for use in the budget-making process. Within 30 days, despite all this careful preparation, another wave of uncontrollable enthusiasm had swept through the legislature.

"Wonders never cease," Drury wrote in the April edition of News & Views. "The governor's budget totalled over $35 million for state parks—close to one-half of our Five Year Master Plan. But the assembly added over $9 million in park items, making a total of $44,-174,528. This was close to ten times our budget of a few years ago. Then it went to the usually conservative and economy-minded senate, which eliminated a few items, but added others and came up with a total of $44,852,762 —even greater than the assembly total.

"In addition, both houses approved

Right: *Columbia State Historic Park.* Below: *Malakoff Diggins State Historic Park.*

items of appropriation from park funds for extraneous purposes of almost $15 million on what might be termed a 'lend-lease' basis. These included $5 million for the 1960 Olympic Games winter development at Squaw Valley, $7.28 million for flood relief, and $2.5 million for a parking area at the Los Angeles Stadium. From the net proceeds of these three projects the park and beach funds may in due course be reimbursed. Thus the total appropriated from park funds this session was in the neighborhood of $59 million."

The wooden-hulled, three-masted lumber schooner C. A. Thayer in Puget Sound preparing for her final voyage southward, (October 1957) to become part of San Francisco Maritime State Historic Park.

Despite some reservations about the unexpected additions to the park budget, Governor Knight approved the whole package, which included $31 million for outright land acquisition—no matching required. The new budget created an unprecedented opportunity for accomplishment, but as Drury and others were well aware, it also constituted a tremendous challenge, for state government was becoming more and more elaborate. Each year more checks and balances, more restraints, were built in to state procedures, and it became more difficult to get things done.

Land acquisition matters, for example, had become a bureaucratic nightmare. Every parcel of land, whether it was worth ten dollars or ten million dollars, had to go through a complicated process that could take years to complete: every proposed acquisition had to be carefully worked out on the staff level before it could be submitted to the State Park Commission; an appropriation bill prepared by the Division of Beaches and Parks had to be approved by the Department of Finance and the Department of Natural Resources before it could be submitted to the legislature. Discussion by various committees of the legislature was often prolonged and detailed. But even after the legislature approved an appropriation bill, and after the governor had signed it, a long process *still* remained to be completed before an owner could be paid and the transaction completed. Some of the steps in that process were likely to involve months or even years of delay.

As supervisor of land acquisition for the Division of Beaches and Parks during the 1950s and early 1960s, Everett Powell was the man who had to keep the process moving. Bright, determined, hard-working, greatly admired for his ability to get things done, Powell enjoyed every phase of his long career in the State Park System. On many occasions, however, he found the acquisition program extremely frustrating. The trouble, as he said later, was that "*everybody* wanted a finger in the pie.

"We'd send a project of ours to the Department of Finance for their approval and instead of looking at it in a strictly financial way they'd send a man out into the field to determine whether or not it was desirable. Now, how was one of their staff members, a man unversed in parks, park acquisition, or anything of a real estate nature, qualified to tell us over in Beaches and Parks whether we should buy it or not— whether it was suitable for park use? And yet, we ran into that all the time. Constantly. They would send somebody out to look at it, and then the finance director's office, of course, would want to have a look at it.

"We had to go through the Department of Finance in order to get on the agenda of the Public Works Board. But even after we got something on the agenda, time after time it would be way down at the bottom and they would postpone it. They would get half way through the agenda, run out of time and put the item over to the next meeting a month later. Sometimes it would go on like that for as much as a year."

Drury himself felt that he had too many bosses: the governor and his staff, the director of Natural Resources, the State Park Commission, and, of course, both houses of the legislature including various interim committees. In Drury's opinion, some legislative committees were actually usurping the

San Francisco Maritime State Historic Park.

90

Manhattan State Beach, one of many popular south coast beaches in the State Park System.

functions of the administrative arm of government, passing judgment on the architectural details of proposed park structures, for example. But even within the administrative branch of state government there were, as Drury later put it, "watchers to watch the watchers." Drury especially disliked the carte blanche veto power held by the Department of Finance. The director of finance, Drury later lamented, could hold up any expenditure he did not view to be in the best interests of the state without hearing or presentation of evidence.

Despite any and all difficulties, however, $4.3 million worth of land was acquired for park purposes in 1956, and other aspects of the state park program also made tremendous progress after the tidelands and offshore oil royalty funds became available. Legislative interest in the park program continued at a high level in 1957 when the legislature once again approved the parks budget and then went on to add still more projects to the 40 already approved in 1956 as part of the five-year acquisition and development program. In fact, one of the most difficult and

trying tasks undertaken by Drury and others during this time was to *limit* the number of projects and the amount of money appropriated to a level that was consistent with reality and good judgment. It was impossible for the Division of Beaches and Parks to do everything at once and even though money was available and staff capability was being expanded, some things (acquisition, for example) simply took time.

In response to pressure for additional spending that was then being brought to bear on the State Park System by various interests, especially

Vikingsholm, a meticulously accurate, privately constructed replica of a 9th century Norse fortress, now part of Emerald Bay State Park.

The Big Sur Coast, Julia Pfeiffer Burns State Park.

*Coralina Cove,
Montana de Oro
State Park.*

recreation-oriented groups in southern California, the legislature provided funding in 1957 for a comprehensive study of recreation needs in California. This three-year project was to result in a specific and detailed plan that would indicate how all levels of government could work together most effectively to meet California's overall recreation needs. Drury hoped that the plan, which was to be known as the "California Public Outdoor Recreation Plan," would at least clarify two things: (1) the difference between state park responsibilities and those of cities, counties, and other local agencies; and (2) the difference between recreational use of man-made reservoirs on the one hand, and park-style preservation of natural areas or historic sites on the other. The study got underway in October 1957 when Elmer Aldrich was named executive officer to coordinate the work on behalf of a high-level interagency committee.

Political Cross-Currents

Although the legislature was generous in its support of the State Park System during the late 1950s, there were a great many political cross-currents at work, some of which threatened to derail the program or undo earlier accomplishments. In 1957, for example, Senate Concurrent Resolution 128 "directed" the State Park Commission to permit grazing in Anza-Borrego Desert, Palomar, and Cuyamaca Rancho State Parks. Though this resolution lacked the force of law, it did indicate senate sympathy toward grazing interests at the expense of park values, even in the face of clearly stated park commission opposition. Senate Bill 378 of that same year would have had even more disastrous results, for it would have greatly limited the commission's right to eminent domain, thereby crippling the park acquisition program. This bill was approved by the legislature but vetoed by Governor Knight.

Along with these and many other threats to the integrity and continued growth of the State Park System, there was an increasing public and legislative impatience with the state park land acquisition program. As Drury said at one point, "No proponent of any project has yet been found who is recon-

*Native grasses,
Sonoma Coast
State Beach.*

A six-minute "home movie" by Ken Murray is shown to tour groups. The film features movie stars and other famous visitors to San Simeon during the 1920s and 30s. Shown here: Clark Gable, Carole Lombard, and Hearst himself.

Hearst San Simeon State Historical Monument. A gift to the people of California from the Hearst Corporation in memory of William Randolph Hearst and his mother, Phoebe Apperson Hearst.

ciled to its acquisition in other than the first year of the Five Year Master Plan." This was true even though the legislature itself had approved the division's five-year plan, and even though the division could point to steady accomplishment within the framework of that plan. Nevertheless, many legislators found it difficult or impossible to abide by the established priorities. Instead of waiting and working through the statewide planning process, they submitted individual acquisition bills.

"If I ever had any ambitions to enter a popularity contest they were blasted by that one circumstance," Drury later said, "because it was my unhappy lot to go before the legislative committees, and making every attempt to be fair and candid, tell them which of these bills embodied projects that were in our five-year program, and which did not. This was a most unenviable position to be in. As some of them said to me,

'It's just possible that you might not be infallible'—which I was frankly willing to admit, and which, before we were through, I recognized fully."

These and other controversial matters that came along toward the end of Drury's tenure as chief of the Division of Beaches and Parks made for some tempestuous moments. But Drury's dip-

lomatic manner never faltered. Through it all he retained not only his principles and ideals, but also his wonderful sense of humor and his ability to enjoy his work on behalf of the public.

In April 1959, Newton Drury reached the age of 70—mandatory retirement age for state service. In announcing his retirement he said that he had "mingled feelings" of regret and gratitude: regret that he would be leaving many associations that he valued highly; gratitude that a sound state park program had been developed and was operating effectively in loyal and capable hands. He pointed out that 16 new parks had been created since the five-year masterplan had been put into effect in 1956, and that the system was now made up of 150 parks, beaches, and historical monuments. Altogether these park areas comprised a total of 615,000 acres, and had a book value of $73 million. It was, he said, the fastest growing state park system in the nation and all indications were that its rapid growth would continue.

"I am confident," he said, "that the record will show that we have lived up to our obligations as trustees for this estate. Our program as outlined in the Five-Year Master Plan at the half-way point is well ahead of schedule. It has been a privilege and an outstanding adventure to have worked...in this cause for California's future."

Though he was unaware of it at the time, of course, Drury was far from through with his work on behalf of California's future. In April 1959 his brother Aubrey was still serving as secretary of the Save-the-Redwoods League. Aubrey died in October 1959, however, and Newton Drury decided to return to active duty with the league, which he continued to serve in a lively and productive way for another 19 years, adding still another phase to his already distinguished career. His death in December 1978 at the age of 89 marked the end of an era.

Newton B. Drury, 1959.

Newton Drury and Robert Coon inspecting the old Bale Mill in Napa County about 1955. The Bale Mill finally became part of Napa Valley State Park in 1973.

8 Parks and the New Conservation

Changing Times

"Something will have gone out of us as a people if we ever let the remaining wilderness be destroyed.... Without any remaining wilderness we are committed wholly, without chance for even momentary reflection and rest, to a headlong drive into our technological termite-life, the Brave New World of a completely man-controlled environment."

Wallace Stegner, 1960

In November 1958, for only the second time in the 20th century, a Democrat was elected governor of California. In his inaugural address in January 1959 the new governor, Edmund G. "Pat" Brown, promised to follow "the path of responsible liberalism...and the giant footsteps" of earlier progressive governors including the Republicans Hiram Johnson and Earl Warren. This was non-partisan rhetoric, of course, but the fact was that for the first time in 80 years, Democrats held a majority of seats in both houses of the legislature as well as the governorship. They had also swept all but one of the other high-level elective positions in state government, and the post-election appointments process brought still more Democrats into state government. Most of these officials were relatively young and quite eager to take charge of programs that had been in Republican hands for many years.

The state park program was no exception. Joseph R. Knowland had been chairman of the State Park Commission ever since 1943. Although he was scrupulously non-partisan in park matters, he was otherwise a well-known and highly partisan politcal figure. According to some observers, he very nearly dominated California Republican politics and was quite important among Republicans on the national level. His close ties to Chief Justice Earl Warren and other leading Republicans were well known. And he was the father of U. S. Senator William F. Knowland, a leading contender for the Repubiican presidential nomination prior to his unsuccessful run for the governorship of California against "Pat" Brown in November 1958. These strong Republican connections made Knowland and the State Park Commission especially interesting to Democrats in the legislature and elsewhere in state government.

Early in 1959, legislation was designed to strip the State Park Commission of its executive and administrative powers and make it strictly an advisory body. This change was recommended simply as an administrative improvement, but it also dramatically diminished the power of commission chairman Joseph R. Knowland, who still had one year left in his current four-year commission term.

In March 1959, Governor Brown made his first two appointments to the State Park Commission: Joseph C. Houghteling of northern California, and Will Rogers, Jr. of southern California. Both men were newspaper publishers; both were personally acquainted with the governor; and both had been active in Democratic politics; both men were effective lobbyists on behalf of the park system. Between them, they managed to obtain legislative approval for bills that ended State Park System dependence on oil royalty funds and returned the park program to the general fund. Legislation also streamlined commission procedures by giving greater executive and administrative power to the chief of the division. With help from Jess Unruh, speaker of the assembly, the Emerald Bay highway problem was returned to committee for "a long period of study." And with concurrence from Knowland and others on the commission, Houghteling and Rogers persuaded the governor to name Charles DeTurk to be chief of the Division of Beaches and Parks replacing Newton Drury, whose retirement was effective May 1.

DeTurk was a landscape architect by training and a career park man who had worked in Pennsylvania, Michigan, and Indiana at city, county, and state levels. He was director of the Indiana State Park System during World War II, and had been an active member of the National Conference on State Parks, serving as president of that organization between 1954 and 1956. His most recent experience was as a park planner in the state of Washington.

At a time when a break with the past seemed appropriate to those in power, DeTurk's out-of-state experience was an asset. He was, moreover, exceedingly charming and well spoken—a persuasive public speaker. Easygoing and friendly, he was willing to let the State Park Commission define the line between administrative matters and policy making.

Despite all the energy and enthusiasm of the new administration, the State Park System continued on its established course throughout 1959. A reorganization and decentralization plan, developed and partly implemented by the previous administration, was completed. The ongoing land acquisition program broke the all-time record for

Sunset near Jenner, Sonoma Coast State Beach.

Charles A. DeTurk.

amount of land purchased in a single year—59,316 acres valued at $6,524,-469. Two entirely new parks were included in this set of accomplishments: Plumas-Eureka and Henry W. Coe State Parks. But, owing to the decline and then complete cutoff of income from oil royalties, the commission was forced to defer action on some $14 million worth of future park projects. This was alarming to many park advocates, because hundreds of thousands of people were still being turned away from the parks each year and demand for park and recreation facilities was steadily increasing.

Throughout 1959 and early 1960 Governor Brown and his top aides were preoccupied with civil rights legislation, revenue matters, and especially the governor's $1.75 billion State Water Project—the largest bond act proposal ever passed by any state for any purpose. But the governor was also interested in parks. He was personally familiar with many of California's state park areas, and was in the habit of taking a pack trip in the mountains each year, usually in the company of Chief Justice Earl Warren, former governor of California. As Joe Houghteling later put it: "Pat Brown had a real feeling for the people of California. He liked people, and he liked parks. And he was convinced that parks were going to be especially important as the state continued to grow. In terms of parks as with other areas of concern, Pat wanted state government to play a dynamic role. He was expansive, a man of great enthusiasm. You could just feel it bubbling over. He was, after all, a Californian, and he had the typical California view that we all had then that things were expanding, that we could buy all the parks, build all the freeways, provide all the water that would be needed for the future."

At Asilomar in September, 1959, as keynote speaker at the 39th annual meeting of the National Conference on State Parks. Governor Brown promised that the Division of Beaches and Parks and the people of California would "not be short-changed on the development of our present state parks and beaches, nor in the acquisition and development of new areas." More specifically, he called for a doubling of the number of state park campsites and new facilities

for swimming, boating, water-skiing, and other forms of recreation that could take advantage of the proposed water project reservoirs. He also called for "vastly stepped-up use of minimum security prison inmates" to help develop the parks. "I also intend," he said, "to see that our internationally famous Squaw Valley, site of the 1960 Winter Olympic Games, is developed as a year-round state park for the benefit of all our citizens, not just for a favored few."

In March 1960, while all of these matters were still pending, Joseph R. Knowland reached the end of his career as a state park commissioner. He was 87 years old, had served on the commission for nearly 25 years, and had been chairman for 20 of those years. In all that time—both on and off the commission, as well as long before the commission had been created—he had played an important role in helping develop the California State Park System into one of the most outstanding in the nation. Rarely had he missed a commission meeting, and rarely had he declined to make himself available for special events or extra assignments such as the chairmanship of the California Centennial Commission in 1948-50, or serving on the California Historical Landmarks Committee. Furthermore, in all his years of public service, he never asked for or accepted any reimbursement for expenses.

He was still alert and able at 87, though he tended to grow weary toward the end of a commission work day. He perceived, however, that the time had come for a change. New problems and challenges were arising, and with the Democrats in power his lines of communication were not as strong as they had once been. He was still highly respected by everyone, but it was time, he felt, for other and younger people to try their hand at the park business. And so, although Governor Brown offered to reappoint him to yet another term, Knowland announced his retirement from the commission.

A Bold and Dynamic Program

Will Rogers, Jr. was named chairman of the State Park Commission in March 1960, and along with Charlie DeTurk

and DeWitt Nelson, was asked by the governor to put together a "bold, dynamic, and detailed program" for future development of the State Park System. Such a plan—in effect, a new five-year plan—was submitted to the governor late in 1960 and subsequently presented to the legislature and the public. Immediate reaction by the press was overwhelmingly favorable. Everyone agreed that the state parks were crowded, that new parks as well as more campsites and other new facilities of all kinds were badly needed. As the study itself pointed out, population of the state had increased by 49 percent in the previous decade, while park acreage had increased only 19 percent. State park attendance meanwhile had increased 359 percent to some 25 million visitor-days. Moreover, the plan seemed to have something in it for everyone. The only question raised in the press or in the legislature was whether it was prudent to spend $150 million on state parks when so many other public programs were also in need of funding, and at a time when state revenues were declining.

As it turned out, despite enthusiastic support from the public and the press, the legislature was unwilling to provide the needed money as requested from the general fund. Some argued that it would be less painful and perhaps more appropriate to finance the program by means of a new bond act. But the Brown administration was reluctant to set up a new form of special funding for parks. Having just rescued the park program from dependence on oil royalties, they preferred to keep it "in the mainstream of state government" by having its entire budget come out of the general fund.

By the end of the legislative session it was clear to everyone, including the governor, that although the ordinary support budget for parks could be taken from the general fund, any large-scale capital improvement program would have to rely on a bond issue. It soon began to appear, moreover, that the proposed $150 million park program would have to be cut down—perhaps in half—and submitted to a vote of the people in 1962. In November 1960, while this matter was being considered, the appropriateness and probable success of such a strategy was underscored when voters in the state of New York approved a $75 million bond proposal by a three to one margin. A year later, New Jersey voters overwhelmingly approved $60 million worth of bonds for state and local park acquisition purposes. At the same time, San Francisco voters decided (two to one) to spend $1.25 million to acquire Fort Funston, a scenic ocean-front area which, as a United States military base, had long been off limits to the public.

With all signs seeming so favorable, Senate Bill 2 was submitted and quickly passed by the legislature in early 1962. Signed by the governor on April 15, the bill called for a referendum to appear on the June primary ballot that would let the people of California vote for or against a $150 million State Park and Recreation bond act. A few weeks later, however, on June 5, 1962, voters rejected the proposal by a narrow margin —1,886,915 to 1,693,704. Charles De-Turk noted shortly afterward that the campaign on behalf of the bond act had been so brief that many people never really learned what it was all about. For lack of information, many people—13 percent of the voters in that election—simply did not vote either for or against the park bonds. Ironically, he said, favorable publicity about the bond act had been more plentiful *after* the election than before it.

Overruling some of his advisors, Governor Brown soon decided that the park bond question should be put to the voters again, and as soon as possible. One outspoken advocate of such a strategy was State Park Commissioner Harold Zellerbach of San Francisco. As his fellow commissioner Joe Houghteling remembered it, "Zellerbach was persistent. I would go to the governor and give my opinion. But he would say, *'Now Pat, you've got to do it. Don't give me any excuses. Its got to be on the ballot.'* Harold was that sort of guy —a real fighter for whatever he believed in."

Zellerbach and Houghteling, chairman of the commission from May 1961 to January 1963, as well as other park bond advocates, agreed that the new bond proposal should be scheduled for the November 1964 general election. Such a schedule would provide plenty of time for a thorough campaign on behalf of the bonds. Meanwhile, as detailed plans and proposals for the bond program were put together, a number of events occurred both in California and throughout the nation that increased the probability of success.

The "New Conservation"

Throughout the 1960s a growing number of people throughout the country were dismayed and even alarmed by what was happening to the quality of the American environment. Urbaniza-

tion and industrialization were proceeding rapidly, and problems in California were further complicated by steady population increases as a result of large-scale in-migration. Nearly three million people from other parts of the nation moved to California between 1950 and 1960—more than arrived in the entire United States from other parts of the world during that same period. Moreover, much of the new urban growth was automobile- and highway-oriented, the result of massive highway construction subsidies provided by the state and national governments. The Federal Highway Act of 1956 provided funding for some 41,000 miles of new highway. And as the planners of the act themselves pointed out, the intent of this program was to "disperse our factories, our stores, our people; in short, to create a revolution in living habits." This proposed "revolution" worried many observers; it was happening so fast that people had little chance to evaluate its intention, or learn to cope with its effects. The State of California alone was spending a million dollars a day on highway construction, and was planning to spend $10 billion on some 12,500 miles of new highway within the next 20 years.

As many saw it, the major drawback to this kind of automobile-oriented planning and growth was that it did not take general social and environmental factors into consideration. It was single-purpose planning, whose generally intended but unplanned by-product was a massive diffusion of urban growth — "sprawl" — that consumed vast areas of land, some of which was vitally needed for agriculture and other open space uses including parks and recreation. As the eminent sociologist William H. Whyte, Jr. described it in 1958 in an article that appeared in the *New York Herald Tribune:* "Already huge patches of once green countryside have been turned into vast, smog-filled deserts that are neither city, suburb nor country, and each day—at a rate of some 3,000 acres a day—more countryside is being bulldozed under." In some parts of the country, Whyte pointed out, "the subdivisions of one city are beginning to meet up with the subdivisions of another."

The situation was not hopeless, according to Whyte. Literally countless

Cartoon used in the 1962 State Park Bond Act campaign.

CLOSE THE GATE BEFORE THE HORSE IS STOLEN

In the winter of 1955-56 and again in December 1964, severe flood damage occurred along the Eel River and its tributaries. Damage was especially severe in areas downstream from intensive logging. At Humboldt Redwoods State Park the upper Bull Creek watershed (outside the park) had been stripped of its native forest; downstream (within the park) 600 old-growth redwoods were destroyed. Thereafter, in order to protect natural values in forested areas, emphasis was given to acquiring complete watersheds.

local efforts were being made "by private and public groups to control sprawl and save open space. But each group is going at the problem from its special point of view, indeed without even finding out what the other groups are up to, the groups often acting more as antagonists than as allies—and all go down to piecemeal defeat." Once the various groups are persuaded of their mutual interest, he prophesied, "they will become a pressure group of great effectiveness."

In California, and across the nation, planning and conservation groups were indeed already growing and coalescing into new, more sophisticated, and ever stronger alliances. Membership in the Sierra Club, for example, doubled between 1950 and 1960, and then doubled again between 1960 and 1965. And new organizations—most of them local, ad hoc groups—sprang up in unprecedented numbers. Several statewide environmental planning and conservation organizations also were created in the early and mid-1960s. California Tomorrow, for example, was organized by Alfred E. Heller and others in 1961, and shortly afterward produced two books, *California Going, Going . . .* and *Phantom Cities of California,* which described California's environmental problems in lucid and compelling terms. These books covered a wide range of local and statewide issues from freeway planning and agricultural land preservation to air pollution, water pollution, and general "uglification." Together with California Tomorrow's quarterly magazine, *Cry California,* they argued persuasively that despite many small, valiant efforts by public-spirited citizens, the bright and promising California landscape was being defiled, and the future of California—environmentally, socially, and economically—was being seriously compromised by runaway growth and haphazard development.

This vastly broadened set of interests on the part of the conservation movement, not just in California but all across the nation, was later referred to by President Lyndon B. Johnson as "the new conservation." "For centuries," the President said in a speech to Congress in February 1965, "Americans have drawn strength and inspiration from the beauty of our country. It would

be a neglectful generation indeed, indifferent alike to the judgment of history and the command of principle, which failed to preserve and extend such a heritage for its descendants. Yet the storm of modern change is threatening to blight and diminish in a few decades what has been cherished and protected for generations." A new conservation movement was needed, the president said, to deal with the new problems of urban blight and crowding and what he called "the darker side" of modern technology whose "uncontrolled waste products are menacing the world we live in, our enjoyment and our health.

"What a citizen sees every day is his America. If it is attractive it adds to the quality of his life. If it is ugly it can degrade his existence. . . . We must [therefore] not only protect the countryside and save it from destruction, we must restore what has been destroyed and salvage the beauty and charm of our cities. . . . Beauty must not be just a holiday treat, but a part of our daily life."

While the conservation movement of the 1960s grew and broadened to include a wide range of environmental issues, its park and wilderness preservation objectives also enjoyed unprecedented success. Under Presidents Kennedy and Johnson, the National Park System was greatly expanded, and in 1964, after an eight-year campaign on its behalf, the Wilderness Act was finally approved. The act applied directly to millions of acres of America's remaining wilderness, but as novelist and university professor Wallace Stegner said while testifying on behalf of the Wilderness Act, the symbolic and philosophical implications of the act were far broader: "What I want to speak for," Stegner said, "is not so much the wilderness uses, valuable as those are, but the wilderness *idea* which is a resource in itself. . . . Something will have gone out of us as a people if we ever let the remaining wilderness be destroyed. . . . For an American, insofar as he is new and different at all, is a civilized man who has renewed himself in the wild. The American experience has been the confrontation of old peoples and cultures by a world as new as if it had just arisen from the sea. That gave us our hope and our

excitement, and the hope and excitement can be passed on to newer Americans; Americans who never saw any phase of the frontier. But only so long as we keep the remainder of our wild as a reserve and a promise. . . .''

President Johnson signed the Wilderness Act into law on September 3, 1964. On that same day he also signed legislation that had originally been sponsored by John F. Kennedy in 1962, calling for the creation of a Land and Water Conservation Fund designed to make federal money available to the states for park and recreation purposes. This money—a projected $150 million per year—was to come from use fees charged at federal recreation areas, and from other related sources. (One year later, on September 27, 1965, California became the first state to have its outdoor recreation plan approved for funding under the Land and Water Conservation Act.)

These landmark decisions by Congress and the president, and the campaigns that led up to them, as well as the phenomenal growth of the conservation movement in general and the unprecedented number of books and articles on environmental matters that appeared during the early 1960s, all helped set the tone for California's next ambitious step forward in terms of parks and recreation.

The 1964 Bond Act

Early in 1963 state Senator Ronald Cameron and Speaker of the Assembly Jess Unruh introduced legislation calling for a $150 million state park and recreation bond act to go before the voters in November 1964. "We are facing a very serious recreational crisis," they told their fellow legislators. "The supply of suitable lands for recreation is fast disappearing. Should we fail to act now to buy and set aside land which we will need for park and recreation purposes it will be lost to us forever."

In an April 1963 message to the legislature, Governor Brown made it clear that he fully supported the new bond proposal. Referring to the June 1962 rejection of a similar proposal he said: "That defeat, it is now generally conceded, did not reflect any refusal of the California electorate to meet our

VOTE YES ON

1

PROPOSITION ONE

urgent needs for beaches and parks. It resulted from the facts that there were too many bond proposals on a single ballot; the proposal itself was complex; and further, there was insufficient time to make a proper presentation of the issues to the people of California."

The governor also pointed out that an interim, emergency appropriation was needed because the new bond proposal could not be presented to the people before November 1964. "In the meantime," he said, "more land—especially irreplaceable beach property—will inevitably be lost unless we take action at this session." He therefore proposed emergency legislation to provide $19 million with which the state could acquire two new parks and add to 19 existing park units. The land to be acquired amounted to some 25,200 acres of prime beach and park property including "eight miles of ocean frontage now barred to the public." The governor indicated that all of this land might be "lost to the people as a result of mushrooming subdivisions and rising prices," whereas acquisition of the land for park purposes would permit the development of "2,100 picnic areas and 6,300 overnight camp sites—nearly enough to double the present resources."

With the sentiment for parks and for general environmental protection and improvement rising to unprecedented heights, the legislature approved both the emergency funding proposal and enabling legislation for the new bond act. On July 15, 1963, Governor Brown happily signed both pieces of legislation. There was no hint of overconfidence, however, among supporters of the park bond issue. The defeat of the 1962 park bonds was still fresh in everyone's memory, and many observers, including the governor, feared that a second failure might permanently damage the park movement. Supporters of the bond act, therefore, set out to avoid the mistakes that had been made in 1962.

The first significant step to ensure passage of the 1964 bond act was taken while Senate Bill 153—the Cameron-Unruh Beach, Park, Recreational, and Historical Facilities Bond Act of 1964—was still going through the legislature during the spring of 1963. Once the bill had been approved by the state

senate in roughly its original (1962) form, a group of leading legislators, legislative staff members, and representatives of the governor's office got together to weed out any features that might make the proposal objectionable, not just to the assembly, but to the electorate who would be asked to approve it at the polls in November 1964. Changes in the bill included the deletion of a number of "pet projects" that had been inserted while the bill was going through the senate. Stronger guidelines for expending the funds were added in order to eliminate or at least minimize future "pork-barrel" influences. Money for small craft harbors was deleted, and more funds were provided for grants to local park and recreation agencies. This feature implied the creation of a whole new function of state government—state support for local park and recreation agencies—and thus marked the inauguration of what has become a very important part of the park movement in California.

The result of all these changes was a bill that all of the conferees including both authors, Jesse M. Unruh and Ronald Cameron, felt would have a good chance of succeeding at the polls. Those who worried about senate concurrence in the amended bill were reassured by Senator Cameron who asked that the matter be left in his hands. Cameron then simply held on to the amended bill until the very last moments of the last session of that year's legislature, when, among the usual last-minute rush of action prior to adjournment, SB153 was unanimously approved without debate.

The campaign for public support of the 1964 bond act got underway in the autumn of 1963 when "Californians for Beaches and Parks" was formed, funds were raised, a small campaign staff was hired, and a campaign strategy approved by an informal conference committee made up of 17 people including legislators, state park commissioners, and other interested parties. Ray King, a legislative consultant and man-about-politics, was hired to coordinate the campaign. While serving as a consultant to the Assembly Committee on Natural Resources, Planning, and Public Works, King had helped draft the revised bond act legislation. He was, therefore, already familiar with

the issues and well known to most park bond advocates.

The campaign itself was split into two parts. The first phase was strictly educational. Current park problems and the need for an expanded state park program were described without reference to the forthcoming ballot issue. This phase of the campaign was coordinated by the Sierra Club, whose leaders checked first with the attorney general and the Internal Revenue Service to make certain that such participation would not conflict with the club's nonprofit, tax-exempt status. This phase of the campaign continued for about seven months and was then followed by an all-out political effort handled entirely by Californians for Beaches and Parks. Frank Jordan, the secretary of state, agreed to place the park bond issue first on the ballot, and the campaign began to focus on getting people to "Vote Yes on Proposition One."

Fund-raising efforts to support the campaign were led by Harold Zellerbach, whose early involvement got the campaign off to an energetic start. Soon Edwin W. Pauley agreed to serve as chairman of a southern California finance committee, but even then sufficient funds were not available for the entire campaign — even as originally projected on a "bare-bones" basis. This lack of funds was counterbalanced, however, by several very special gifts. Walt Disney not only endorsed the bond act (though he ordinarily opposed all bond proposals), he agreed to be on the executive board of Californians for Beaches and Parks, and his film studio produced a 14-minute color movie that played a central role in the campaign. Shown to countless organizations by a speakers bureau that eventually included some 200 volunteers, the film was also shown on TV, in commercial movie houses as a between-features "short," and at evening campfire programs in the state parks.

The 14-minute film described the park system and its problems but did not mention the bond act. Disney, however, also did a TV "spot" or short "commercial" — a 54-second sales pitch—on behalf of Proposition One, as did Janet Leigh, the famous movie actress who was then serving on the State Recreation Commission. These contributions as well as others (office

In 1956 the Save-the-Redwoods League set out to acquire the entire upper Bull Creek watershed as a step toward protecting the Rockefeller Forest in Humboldt Redwoods State Park. By February 1963 the league had acquired 13,558 acres—about two-thirds of the necessary area. Here, Newton Drury and Walter A. Starr are describing the area and presenting Governor Edmund G. Brown with gift deeds for land valued at approximately $1 million.

space for a year, office equipment and furniture for a year, free use of rental cars, etc.) made it possible to mount an effective campaign with a minimum of cash.

The governor used the prestige of his office and expressed his own personal enthusiasm for the park bond issue in many ways. Early in the campaign he invited radio and television station representatives from throughout the state to a luncheon at the governor's mansion and asked all of them to endorse the bond issue. In October, when time and space in the media were hard to get because of competition from the presidential and other political campaigns, the governor arranged for a special "press-lift" such as he had used with great success during his 1962 gubernatorial campaign. A large privately owned airplane (donated to the cause) carried former governor Goodwin Knight, Assembly Speaker Jesse Unruh, and several other state senators and assemblymen on a three-day tour of the state with press conferences at airports along the way and special breakfast and luncheon gatherings. The governor himself joined the festivities at the last stop. News coverage of this tour was excellent and more than made up for any lack of paid advertising.

The "press-lift" itself and the campaign in general were handled on a thoroughly non-partisan basis so that newspaper, radio, and TV editors, and others were able to endorse and otherwise support the bond act. In fact, as had been the case in 1928, most of the media people and most local chambers of commerce throughout the state endorsed the bond act, as did all but a handful of important statewide organizations.

On November 3, 1964, for the second time in the history of the state, the people of California voted overwhelmingly for a park system bond issue. The final vote revealed that the bonds had pased with a plurality of over 1.5 million votes—3,864,673 to 2,345,881.

After the Election

The first order of business after passage of the bond act was to complete all of the many feasibility studies of potential park, beach, and historic areas as called for by the legislature. A total of 19 of these studies were scheduled for completion by early 1965, but those who had worked so hard on the bond campaign — legislators and others including Harold Zellerbach—soon began to feel that the whole process was moving far too slowly. Charles DeTurk, director of the Department of Parks and Recreation, was universally admired as a very gentle and likable man, but some observers were convinced that he simply wasn't able to be tough when toughness was required; he wouldn't fight for what he believed in, either with his own staff or with others including members of the legislature. In mid-December, word reached DeTurk that he would have to step aside and let someone else have a crack at getting the bond act acquisition program moving.

Winner of the scramble to replace DeTurk was an ambitious young man by the name of Fred L. Jones whose background was not in parks, but in wildlife management. Because of his experience in the Department of Fish and Game, and because of his three-year stint as assistant to the Administrator of the Department of Natural Resources, Jones was familiar in a general way with state park matters. His primary qualification as a replacement for DeTurk, however, was that he was ready, willing, and able to take charge, to be decisive.

The State Park System's administrative hierarchy had been revised in 1961 when the old Division of Beaches and Parks merged with the Division of Recreation and the Division of Small Craft Harbors to form the new Department of Parks and Recreation. At that time DeTurk had "moved up" from the old position of chief of the Division of Beaches and Parks to the new position of director of the Department of Parks and Recreation. The old position continued to exist, however, and was filled for three years by Ed Dolder. Now in March 1965, DeTurk moved back to his old position as chief, saying simply that he had been losing touch with the work that meant most to him and that he had requested an opportunity to go back to his old job. Dolder was appointed special consultant and later chief deputy to the new director and was assigned to work on matters pertaining to the recently approved bond act.

These changes in top-level personnel, and the subsequent chain reaction all through the Department of Parks and Recreation, had a profound impact on the individuals involved, but did not basically alter the frustratingly slow and unwieldly process involved in acquiring land for state park purposes. The availability of 1964 bond funds, and the 1963 emergency acquisition funds —or "opportunity funds" as they came to be called—did eventually result in the creation of new parks as well as significant additions to many older park areas.

New parks that date from this time include the Forest of Nisene Marks State Park in 1963; Sugarloaf Ridge State Park, Smithe Redwoods State Reserve, and Bidwell Mansion State Historic Park in 1964; Montana de Oro State Park, and Malakoff Diggins State Historic Park in 1965; Sugar Pine Point and Point Mugu State Parks in 1966. It should be noted, however, that these areas were not acquired simply as the result of routine expenditures of public funds.

Public acquisition of many new park areas would have been impossible without the spirited cooperation and, in some cases, the inspirational leadership and generous financial support of private citizens and special organizations. The Forest of Nisene Marks, 10,000 acres of handsome second-growth redwoods on Aptos Creek in Santa Cruz County, was acquired by means of a $1.4 million gift from Herman, Andrew, and Agnes Marks. A development firm had offered them several million dollars for the land, but they preferred to see the area preserved for public use as a way of keeping alive the spirit of their mother, Nisene. This wonderful gift to the people of California was arranged by Herman Marks and state park planner and administrator Charles Mehlert, with the help of Dick and Doris Leonard, Dorothy Varian, George Collins and the other visionary and idealistic citizens who made up Conservation Associates and the Monterey chapter of the Nature Conservancy. The half-million dollars of "opportunity funds" used to complete this acquisition constituted the first practical application of the $19 million emergency acquisition fund ap-

Fred L. Jones.

William Penn Mott, Jr.

proved in 1963.

Smaller but nevertheless essential financial contributions from private citizens and groups were involved in the acquisition of Bidwell Mansion in Chico, and Sugarloaf Ridge in Sonoma County. Such contributions were no longer required for matching purposes as they had been prior to 1956, but they very often made the crucial difference in determining the feasibility of a park acquisition project.

Perhaps the most spectacular addition to an existing park during this period was that of Gold Bluff Beach, an addition to Prairie Creek Redwoods State Park in Humboldt County. The area included some four and one-half miles of ocean frontage backed by towering bluffs and a magnificent

mixed conifer forest. Free-roaming elk made the area especially appealing as a wilderness landscape. Preservation of this scenic area and its associated wildlife was made possible by the Save-the-Redwoods League, which provided more than $1 million of the $2.4 million needed to acquire the area from the Pacific Lumber Company in 1965. While completing this transaction early in 1966, Governor Brown noted that in the years since its formation, the league had contributed some $12 million to redwood forest preservation projects on behalf of the people of the state and the nation.

By December 1966, after the $8.2 million expenditure for Sugar Pine Point at Lake Tahoe and the $15.4 million expenditure for land at Point Mugu,

roughly half the 1964 bond funds available for state park acquisition was used up—*but only ten of the 100 projects* proposed for consideration by the legislature had been approved and funded. Meanwhile, an independent survey indicated that some 1.5 million people were being turned away from the state parks each year for lack of space and facilities. In a 1966 report to the governor, parks director Fred Jones indicated that $500 million would have to be spent over the following 20 years if the state was going to solve the turn-away problem and adequately meet the growing demand for park and recreation opportunities.

William Penn Mott, Jr.

Another far-reaching shift in state government occurred after November 1966 when Governor "Pat" Brown was defeated in his bid for re-election by the Republicans under Ronald Reagan. In his inaugural address on January 5, 1967, Reagan set the tone of the new administration when he announced that in his opinion the unduly high cost of state government was having an adverse effect on the business climate. Therefore, he said, "We are going to squeeze and cut and trim until we reduce the cost of government." Government spending and government programs had a legitimate role to play in solving problems, he explained, but sometimes government spending and new programs were not the right answer. Sometimes the best result came simply from government "taking the lead in mobilizing the full and voluntary resources of the people. In California we call this partnership between the people and government the Creative Society."

In the eyes of the new governor and his top advisors, one person stood out head and shoulders above all others as a candidate for the position of director, California Department of Parks and Recreation. William Penn Mott, Jr. had begun his career in park work in 1933 as a landscape architect with the National Park Service. From there he had gone on to demonstrate unusual ability as a park executive and as an expert at "mobilizing the full and voluntary

Fern Canyon. Part of the Gold Bluff Beach-Fern Canyon addition to Prairie Creek Redwoods State Park, 1965.

William Penn Mott, Jr. (far left) at Rubicon Point, September 1935. Inspecting CCC projects for the National Park Service.

resources of the people." As superintendent of parks in Oakland, California, between 1946 and 1962, he had brought new vitality to the city's park program based in large part on voluntary contributions of time, money, and other support from private citizens and groups of every description. Older parks had been repaired and remodeled. New parks and new programs had been created. Children's Fairyland, the Garden Center, an outstanding naturalist program, and the Nature Center at Lake Merritt had all been brought about through the kind of creative partnership between government and the private sector that Governor Reagan praised so highly in his inaugural address.

Moreover, in 1962 Mott had become general manager of the East Bay Regional Park District, which he reorganized, revitalized, and expanded in dramatic and lasting ways. Once again private contributions to the program—roughly $100,000 per year—played an important role in Mott's administration. He had been offered the State Park System director's job in 1959 and again in 1965, but on both occasions he had turned it down in order to complete the projects he had underway in Oakland and the East Bay. In January 1967, however, he was ready to accept Governor Reagan's offer and the challenge that it represented.

Retrenchment, hiring freezes, and 10 percent across-the-board budget cuts were the order of the day in state government, but in his characteristically energetic and enthusiastic manner, Mott announced that the Department of Parks and Recreation would be "entering into a new era of growth and progress with broader responsibilities." The keynote of his administration, he said, would be a tireless pursuit of the highest possible quality both in terms of projects and programs. "We will not compromise quality for quantity, or excellence for mediocrity. Creativity and imagination will be stressed... in all functions of the Department."

Quality in park matters for Bill Mott

was synonymous with professionalism. The public would not accept second-rate parks or support a second-rate park program. The department needed reorganization and a new long-range masterplan, both of which were politically sensitive matters. Mott nevertheless told the governor that he would approach these issues from a strictly professional point of view. The governor's response, as Mott later remembered it, was simple and direct: "Fine," he said. "That's exactly why I'm asking you to take this job. I'll handle the politics and you handle the Department of Parks and Recreation."

In the spring of 1967, acting on the strong mandate given him by the governor, Mott assigned top priority to reorganizational matters. The legislative session was already well advanced when he assumed his responsibilities as director in mid-March, but enabling legislation was nevertheless submitted

and quickly approved, so that before the year was out basic reorganization was an accomplished fact. The seven-member Park Commission and seven-member Recreation Commission held their last meetings in November 1967 and were then replaced by a new, nine-member Park and Recreation Commission chosen from among those who had been serving on the earlier bodies. Along with the difficult diplomatic problems involved in that transition, changes in organizational structure were also the order of the day. The Division of Beaches and Parks and the Division of Recreation were merged within the Department of Parks and Recreation. The Division of Small Craft Harbors moved out of the department and became an entirely separate governmental function that eventually became known as the Department of Boating and Waterways.

Organizational changes within the department itself included centralization, which brought various staff experts to the Sacramento headquarters unit from the district offices. The "area concept" grouped individual parks for administrative purposes under area managers who reported in turn to the district superintendents. A Resource

Leonard Penhale preparing exhibits for the natural history museum at Big Basin about 1948. The State Park System's first fully professional museum exhibit preparator, Penhale was also responsible for exhibits in other state parks including the Museum of Natural History at Morro Bay.

In June of each year starting in 1949, a Park Naturalists Conference was held either in Big Basin or Big Sur to launch the summer season. Fourteen seasonal naturalists attended the program in 1954. Back row center: Program coordinator Elmer Aldrich and his assistant Leonard Penhale.

Management and Protection Division was created within the headquarters organization in order to provide better management of both historical resources and natural ecological factors in the parks. The seasonal naturalist program, which relied for the most part on summer employment of school teachers, was phased out after the 1967 summer season in favor of a new interpretive program that relied on permanent full-time park system employees.

Mott felt that some seasonal naturalists looked upon their summer assignments as paid vacations. Moreover, he felt that the time had come for the regular professional ranger staff to handle "public contact" interpretive programs instead of being restricted to maintenance, administrative, and custodial work. To be sure that the career rangers were ready and able to handle interpretive programs in a professional manner, a special training and staff support program was established to provide information, materials, and ad-

Ranger George Leetch, "Mr. Desert" to his many admirers, leads an interpretive walk at Anza-Borrego Desert State Park.

vice about interpretive techniques.

At the same time, the department's public information program was also improved and expanded. An ambitious park folder and interpretive publications program was launched along with an active public information system designed to make the public more aware of the range of facilities and programs provided by the State Park System.

As Mott expressed it, the object of this large-scale public information and interpretive effort was "to build a bridge between the world of the park and the world of the visitor." Statistical studies made it very clear that most park visitors were residents of large, highly developed urban areas. They were visitors, in effect, not only to the particular park they happened to be in, but to the natural and historical conditions preserved by the parks. It was important, therefore, that adequate arrangements be made for the comfort, convenience, and safety of visitors, but it was even more important that park areas not be looked upon simply as inexpensive camping spots on the way to somewhere else. With a moral and emotional intensity reminiscent of Newton Drury at his most compelling, Mott insisted that the educational value of state parks was of paramount importance. Simply preserving scenic, scientific, and historic features was not enough. Park values were to be pointed out, explained, and made relevant to urban dwellers. The park experience was not only to be "refreshing and recreative," it should send people home with "a greater awareness ... of their responsibility to maintain the quality of the environment."

The William Penn Mott, Jr. Training Center

The environmental movement rose to new heights of popular awareness during the late 1960s and early 1970s, but at the same time the nation was trou-

bled by civil unrest. Disillusionment over the war in Vietnam was widespread, and respect for law and for governmental rules and regulations declined. Suddenly, even state park areas were no longer exempt, as they had long been, from criminal activity. A study on "Crime Control in the California State Parks" revealed that a total of 8,000 violations of the law (including 1,400 felonies) were reported within state park areas in fiscal 1967-68. The study recommended the acquisition of new equipment, plus new procedures and an intensive law enforcement training program for all permanent full-time state park rangers. The governor en-

Ranger Curtis Kraft leads an interpretive walk for cross-country skiers at Calaveras Big Trees State Park.

William Penn Mott, Jr. Training Center at Asilomar. Left: *State Park Historian Bob Reese and Director Mott in the Holman Library.* Right: *Administration and classroom building.*

dorsed this program in April 1969, and it was soon put into effect on a state-wide basis.

There had been an attempt to provide law enforcement training for state park rangers as early as 1961 when a few rangers were permitted to sit in on California Highway Patrol training sessions. Right from the beginning, however, it was clear that a more park-oriented training program was needed, and sentiment began to grow among the rangers that the department should have its own training center and its own specially designed training program to cover not only law enforcement but the whole gamut of ranger respon-

sibilities. This idea was given a significant boost in 1966 when the California State Park Rangers' Association formally endorsed the concept of a centralized training program. Responding to the C.S.P.R.A. ("Sea Spray") resolution in 1967, Bill Mott explored the possibility of using the Asilomar Conference Grounds in Pacific Grove as the site for such a program.

The Department of Parks and Recreation had acquired Asilomar in 1956 in order to preserve its long tradition as a refreshing and inspirational setting for educational conferences. The long, often emotional campaign for public acquisition and preservation of Asilo-

mar had been led by Mrs. Bartlett B. Heard, national vice president of the YWCA, which had owned, developed, and operated Asilomar for some 50 years. Arrangements for State Park System acquisition at one-half of market value had been worked out by Senator Fred Farr, Newton Drury, Joseph R. Knowland and others, despite fears on the part of some state officials that Asilomar would be a burden to the taxpayers of the state. Over the years, however, under the imaginative and energetic management of Roma Philbrook, Asilomar not only paid its own way but built up a sizable cash reserve, even while expanding year after year

Peace officer training for state park rangers.

A class in the training center, Asilomar.

to accommodate more people. With its beautiful setting and well established reputation as an educational center, Asilomar seemed like an ideal place to establish a ranger training program.

Centralized state park ranger training began in a modest way in October 1969, when the first course in park management was held in the "Outside Inn," a small cottage at Asilomar. Soon courses covering a wide range of subjects were developed—park maintenance, administration, history and natural history, resource management, interpretive techniques, etc.—and the value of the program became increasingly obvious. Newly hired ranger trainees graduated from the training program (the first state park ranger training program in the nation) with knowledge, practical skills, and an esprit-de-corps that otherwise would have taken years to acquire. At the same time, older park system employees were able to improve their skills, widen their horizons, and generally revitalize their commitment to park system programs and objectives.

In 1971, plans were laid for the creation of new facilities specifically designed to meet the needs of a State Park System training program. Mott reorganized the board of directors of the Asilomar Operating Corporation, and persuaded the new board to use its cash reserve to acquire land and construct the necessary buildings. Along with lodging for 60 park employees, the beautiful new complex included classroom, office, reading room, and library space. The library became an important and useful archive overnight through the extraordinary generosity of Mrs. W. R. (Zena) Holman of Pacific Grove, who donated the Holman Library of California and American History to the State Park System for placement in the new training center. Valued at approximately $750,000, the 3,200-volume library included first editions and rare books, many of which dealt with early exploration and settlement of the west coast, the mission period, the California gold rush, and other aspects of California and American history.

The handsome custom-designed training center opened for use in October 1973 and was formally dedicated in February 1974 as "Asilomar-East Woods, Center for Continuous Learning." In November 1975, however, the State Park and Recreation Commission recommended that the center be renamed the William Penn Mott, Jr. Training Center in recognition of Mott's courageous leadership and vision in establishing the training program and providing for its physical needs at no cost to the taxpayers.

Planning, Development and Acquisition

While he was director of the California Department of Parks and Recreation, Bill Mott was fond of quoting Daniel Burnham, the famous American planner. "Make no little plans," Burnham warned. "They have no magic to stir men's blood and probably themselves will not be realized. Make big plans; aim high in hope and work." Putting this philosophy into action in 1967-68, Mott had a masterplan prepared to guide long-range development of the State Park System. According to this plan, $1.3 billion were going to be needed over the next 20 years in order for the state to meet its responsibility in the field of outdoor recreation. "Use of the State Park System," the report said, "is growing faster than the population, but the system continues to receive less than one-half of one percent of the state's annual budget. Each year crowding at park units gets worse and the number of turnaways increases. Unless substantial funding is forthcoming, the existing park areas will deteriorate from overcrowding."

In presenting this plan to the State Park Commission, the legislature, the governor, and the public, Mott indicated that its specific five-year spending proposals would require some $60 million, a large portion of which would be earmarked for water-related recreation facilities in southern California. New and larger sources of funding would have to be found, however, in order to keep up with more general statewide park and recreation needs. A $200 million bond act was suggested as one means of financing a portion of the 20-year plan.

But even while this ambitious new plan was being discussed, the state was having difficulty completing its earlier goals. The market for state bonds was virtually pre-empted by the continuing sale of state water bonds approved during the Brown administration to finance construction of the $1.75 billion

Governor Ronald Reagan, August 5, 1969, signing the Recreational Trails Bill of that year. With the governor from left to right: Director Mott, Recreational Trails Advisory Committee Chairman Wendell T. Robie, Senator Robert Lagomarsino, and Committeemember Mrs. Jim Bardin.

The historic Governor's Mansion.

Dedication ceremony, San Onofre State Beach, April 1971.
Left to right: Camp Pendleton Marine Base Chief of Staff Colonel
Radics, State Park Commission Chairman Clarice Gilchrist,
Director Mott, Congressman Alphonzo Bell, and State Parks
Foundation Vice-Chairman Arthur Cates.

State Water Project. Moreover, the interest rate that could be paid on state bonds was limited by state law, but due to inflation and other factors, the interest rate on other kinds of bond issues was beginning to make state bonds less attractive than they had been in earlier years. This problem was eventually worked out, but in the meantime, as long as the 1964 bond act program was still unfinished, it was difficult to obtain new money for a new plan.

During these years, however, a number of new parks were acquired without state funds. The Governor's Mansion became a state historic park in 1968 when Governor Ronald Reagan insisted on living elsewhere and asked that the memory-filled 90-year-old building—home to 13 of California's governors—be designated a state historic landmark, open for public tours.

Castle Rock State Park was created in July 1968 when the State Park Commission officially accepted a gift deed to some $750,000 worth of land along the crest of the Santa Cruz Mountains near Big Basin. The 566-acre area had been acquired by the Sierra Club and by the Varian Foundation as a memorial to Russell Varian, and as a fulfillment of Varian's dream that the area should be preserved for park purposes.

State-owned offshore or submerged lands constituted another opportunity to create park and recreation areas without land acquisition funds from the state. The nation's first underwater reserve had been created offshore from the land portion of Point Lobos State Reserve in 1959. In March 1968, in response to growing interest in underwater recreation, an Advisory Board on Underwater Parks and Reserves was appointed and assigned the task of advising the department where other underwater parks and reserves should be established along the California coastline. This program eventually resulted in significant additions to the State Park System including underwater reserves at Torrey Pines State Reserve, Julia Pfeiffer Burns State Park, and Salt Point State Park.

Several miles of prime southern California ocean beach were added to the State Park System in 1971 without benefit of any state park acquisition funds. This was accomplished by means of a lease of surplus federal acreage at

Camp Pendleton, a U. S. Marine Corps training base. Annadel State Park in Sonoma County, also created in 1971, was made possible by a combination of Land and Water Conservation Funds and gifts to the state coordinated by the newly created State Parks Foundation, a nonprofit corporation specifically set up to handle private gifts to the State Park System.

State park development work was also accomplished at no cost to the state during the Mott years by means of concession agreements, the largest of which, signed in November 1969, called for some $2 million worth of facilities to be built at Lake Oroville State Recreation Area.

Some development proposals during the Mott years were controversial. Extensive development of recreational facilities on Angel Island and at Point Mugu, for example, resulted in outspoken protest by hundreds of people who claimed that these state park areas should not be "over-developed." According to many who testified at various public hearings, the primary value of these and other state parks near urban areas came from the contrast they offered to life in the city. Mott, on the other hand, felt that the lack of adequate park opportunities in many urban areas meant that the state should pro-

vide for more intensive use of state parks near those areas. Intensive use, he insisted, could only be handled properly by carefully planned, intensive development. The controversy that ensued was heated and prolonged.

Eventually, some of Mott's most outspoken critics began to call for his replacement as director. Mott managed to survive this attack by scaling down his development proposals for Angel Island, Point Mugu, and elsewhere, and by agreeing to support legislation that more clearly defined the kind and extent of development that was appropriate in various units of the State Park System.

Top: *San Luis Reservoir and San Luis Reservoir State Recreation Area.*
Bottom: *Recreational development at O'Neill Forebay.*

Individual units had been officially classified as parks, reserves, beaches, or recreation areas ever since 1960 when the State Park Commission adopted a classification policy following recommendations from the National Conference on State Parks. In 1961 a slightly modified version of this policy was given the status of law by the state legislature. Now in 1971, with Mott's approval, the classification system was significantly enlarged and its distinctions and limits more clearly specified.

Expenditure of 1964 bond act funds progressed despite painful delays. Lake Oroville was acquired and developed starting in 1967 with the acquisition of 1,000 acres adjacent to the Oroville Dam and Reservoir. Acquisition and preliminary development of Indian Grinding Rock State Historic Park in

Recreational development at Brown's Ravine, Folsom Lake State Recreation Area.

Amador County was celebrated in the summer of 1968, and a new museum was dedicated at Malakoff Diggins State Historic Park. Acquisition of Salt Point and Andrew Molera State Parks was accomplished in 1968, and the long-delayed acquisition of Red Rock Canyon in Kern County finally got underway in 1969.

A modern campground and other public facilities—some of them designed for year-round use—were constructed at Sugar Pine Point, and the park was finally opened to the public in June 1972, nearly seven years after its acquisition.

In November 1970 the lack of funds for further state park land acquisition was eased in one important way when the people of California approved Proposition 20, which provided $60 million for the planning and development of facilities at State Water Project reservoirs. Fish and wildlife programs received $6 million of the total, but the balance was designated for on-shore park and recreation facilities such as campgrounds, picnic sites, parking lots, and boat ramps at the 17 major reservoirs created by the State Water Project. The funds were especially critical to the Department of Parks and Recreation because, although the state was legally obligated to provide such recreational development, no funds had ever been allocated. Unexpended 1964 bond act funds, for example, had long since been earmarked for other purposes.

In the spring of 1971, with financial constraints still frustrating department plans as well as the hopes and dreams of state park enthusiasts in many parts of the state, Assemblyman Ed Z'berg introduced legislation calling for a new $250 million state park bond issue to be placed before the voters in 1972. Z'berg's bill was approved by the legislature but vetoed by the governor on grounds that such a proposal was premature. The following spring, however, the governor agreed to support similar legislation on condition that the matter be held for a vote of the people in June 1974.

Starting with "Traildays 1969" many thousands of volunteers have contributed tens of thousands of hours each year constructing trails in the Forest of Nisene Marks, Castle Rock, and Big Basin Redwoods State Parks. The 33-mile-long "Skyline to the Sea Trail"— built entirely by volunteers—includes overnight camp areas that enable backpackers to take extended trips through the scenic forests of the Santa Cruz Mountains.

The Rise of Volunteerism

Citizen involvement in state park matters reached unprecedented levels during the years Mott served as director of the Department of Parks and Recreation. Such involvement had always been an informal factor in the state park program, but Mott encouraged the formation of officially recognized citizen advisory committees. He also launched a new program in which cooperative associations were created and turned into full-fledged corporations that could contract with the state to provide various kinds of services. This more formal approach to citizen participation made it possible to clarify and strengthen the relationship between paid staff and unpaid volunteer workers who were interested in serving as docents, visitor center attendants, or perhaps as tour or trail guides.

The sale of interpretive publications at book counters staffed by volunteers made it possible for cooperative associations to raise funds for worthwhile park projects and programs. Some cooperative associations began to stage elaborate festivals and other unique fund-raising events in order to provide still more money for park purposes. Even the office-bound departmental headquarters staff in Sacramento got into the volunteer spirit. With the approval of her fellow staff members, for example, Beth Coppedge and the staff of the Resource Management and Protection Division, started charging a little extra for coffee-break supplies so that accumulated funds could be contributed to the acquisition of private inholdings at Anza-Borrego Desert State Park. Over a period of time this and other small-scale fund-raising efforts made it possible for the Anza-Borrego Committee of the Desert Protective Association and other organizations to acquire more than a thousand acres of desert land for inclusion in Anza-Borrego Desert State Park. These accomplishments are just a few of the many that have been brought about by volunteer citizen groups dedicated to serving and improving the State Park System. By 1974, 35 citizen committees were associated with state parks in California, and membership in such groups was increasing steadily.

Sea lions, Ano Nuevo State Reserve.

The State Parks Foundation

Early in 1968 Bill Mott proposed to the governor's cabinet that a nonprofit, private corporation be organized to solicit and receive gifts on behalf of the State Park System. Such a corporation could accept all kinds of gifts and dispose of them in any way it saw fit, subject, of course, to any special conditions imposed by donors. For example, a parcel of land too small or too isolated to use as park land might be accepted by the corporation and resold in order to provide funds for some other state park purpose. The idea appealed to the governor and his advisors, and so the State Parks Foundation was incorporated and held its first board meeting in October 1969 in the governor's office.

One of the earliest gifts the State Parks Foundation was able to pass on to the State Park System was producer-actor-comedian Ken Murray's cinema "Golden Days of San Simeon," which portrayed many of Hollywood's leading celebrities enjoying the lavish hospitality of William Randolph Hearst at San Simeon during the 1920s and '30s. In subsequent years, foundation gifts to the park system have made possible the creation of Annadel State Park in Sonoma County, Los Osos Oaks State Reserve in San Luis Obispo County, the Poppy Reserve in Antelope Valley, Pine Ridge Museum at Henry W. Coe State Park, reconstruction of the fire-ravaged Russian Orthodox chapel at Fort Ross, as well as many additions and improvements to other parks.

Foundation gifts to the park system by early 1979 amounted to some 14,000 acres of land valued in excess of $18 million. Moreover, several new projects were on the drawing board including

The old Russian Orthodox chapel at Fort Ross was completely destroyed by fire, October 5, 1970.

State Parks Foundation Executive Director Robert Howard and William Penn Mott, Jr. stand beside a scale model of the chapel. The foundation led a spirited fund-raising drive that made it possible to rebuild the chapel.

The original Russian chapel bell melted in the fire, but was recast in Belgium using the original metal.

Several thousand people attended the dedication of the rebuilt chapel, June 8, 1974.

As part of California's Bicentennial Celebration of 1969, the State Park System's exhibit trailer, "California 200," was dedicated in Capitol Park and sent out to visit schools and shopping centers throughout the state.

Renamed "The Park Experience" and filled with natural history exhibits, the trailer began a new tour of urban areas in 1974. A dedicated team of rangers, Harry and Paula Morse, managed to communicate with all comers—here with deaf students, California School for the Deaf, Berkeley.

a "Parks of the Future" program in which landscapes that had been damaged either by man or nature would be reclaimed, rebuilt, restored, and made suitable for use as state parks. Deadline for the completion of this visionary program was set for 2028—the 100th anniversary of the creation of the State Park System.

Other Accomplishments

During Mott's years as director, a campsite reservation system was inaugurated —the first of its kind in the nation. A reservation system for tours of Hearst San Simeon State Historical Monument had been an absolute necessity from the time it first opened to the public, and experience with that program led to the development of a similar reservation program for campsites throughout the State Park System. In 1968 the program was handled on a local basis by the individual park units. By 1970, however, the program was centralized and computerized so that campsite reservations could be made in any one of many commercial ticket outlets in cities throughout the state. Despite some early logistic and financial problems with this centralized approach, the computerized reservation program has steadily grown in popularity. For those who can plan ahead, it eliminates the awful but once commonplace experience of traveling to some distant park only to find the campground filled to capacity and the park entrance blocked by a swarm of frustrated campers waiting hopefully for vacancies to develop.

Mott was also successful—after prolonged difficulty—in putting Squaw Valley and its elaborate winter recreation facilities back on the tax rolls. Land ownership patterns, maintenance arrangements, and operating agreements had been adequate to the needs of the 1960 Winter Olympics, but thereafter the state had found it impossible to operate the area at a reasonable cost. In May 1972, therefore, with the approval of the governor and legislature, the site was classified as state surplus property and turned over to the State Office of General Services for sale to the highest bidder.

The department had scarcely dis-

posed of Squaw Valley, however, when the governor asked Mott and the Department of Parks and Recreation to take on another unusual and difficult challenge—management of Cal Expo, the ambitious, modern, year-round version of California's century-old State Fair. Mott accepted this new challenge in March 1973 with his usual exuberance and optimism, announcing that the traditional month-long State Fair would continue to be a major part of the overall Cal Expo program, and that displays of California's world famous agricultural productivity would continue to be a central attraction.

Urban parks and related park programs were given special attention by Mott and the Department of Parks and Recreation starting in the summer of 1967. Earlier state park planners, including Olmsted in the 1920s, had insisted that cities, counties, and other local agencies take *full* responsibility for local park and recreation matters. State Park System enabling legislation in 1927 had therefore expressly prohibited the State Division of Parks from acquiring or even operating state park units within the city limits of incorporated municipalities. This extreme stand was soon modified, of course, and later steps committed the state to further involvement in urban park matters. One such step was the formation of the State Recreation Commission in 1947. Working on behalf of governmental agencies at all levels, the commission was to study recreation needs, establish policy, and "aid and encourage, but not conduct, public recreation activities" throughout California. The $150 million State Park Bond Act of 1964 had provided $40 million for local park and recreation agencies, and the grants and local assistance function of the Department of Parks and Recreation has continued to be an important aspect of state government since that time.

Nevertheless, the riot in Watts in August 1965—one of the most tragic and destructive civil disorders in 20th century America—as well as other continuing symptoms of widespread civil unrest, made it clear that government in general, including state government, had to do more for disadvantaged people in central city areas. In 1967, as the state and nation braced for yet another "long, hot summer," Mott ad-

vised the governor and his cabinet that parks and recreation could play an important role in helping to solve urban problems. In March 1968 President Johnson's National Advisory Commission on Civil Disorders reported that according to its massive, nation-wide study, the lack of park and recreational opportunities ranked among the most important underlying causes of civil unrest. Unemployment and housing grievances ranked first and second in the study; complaints about inadequate education and recreation opportunities tied for third.

In order to develop a more detailed and sophisticated understanding of urban park and recreation problems, a study was undertaken by the Department of Parks and Recreation in cooperation with the League of California Cities and the County Supervisors' Association of California. Completed and presented to the governor in October 1970, the study—entitled "Recreation Problems in the Urban Impacted Areas of California"—documented the fact that central city areas tended to be park deficient, offering inadequate opportunities for free or nominal-cost recreation of any kind. Moreover, it was found, park programs tended to be city-wide, "standard" offerings that did not reflect the ethnic, racial, economic, and age-related diversity of the population. The study therefore recommended a review of all existing park programs, and a new emphasis on providing not only swimming and other athletic opportunities, but also a broader range of cultural and educational activities. Adequate funding for urban park programs was important, according to the report, but to be truly cost-effective, park programs would also have to be responsive to the diverse needs of local communities and special groups within the overall population.

While this study was underway and while more comprehensive implementation measures were being considered, Mott launched a number of special ventures relative to urban park and recreation needs. For one thing, since all units of the State Park System were located outside the urban "core areas" and since many residents of those areas were not even aware of the state parks, Mott decided that an ongoing effort should be made to "take parks

Sand dunes, Pismo Dunes Natural Preserve.

to the people.'' Radio and TV programs and a number of state park publications were produced in Spanish and other languages. A series of recreational outings for inner city children was arranged in cooperation with Amtrak. A 40-foot-long mobile exhibit trailer filled with historical exhibits was designed and built and sent out to tour urban areas throughout the state. This project, funded by a gift from the estate of Ida M. Sbragia of San Francisco, was part of the State Park System's contribution to the celebration of the 200th anniversary of the Spanish occupation of California. After visiting schools and parks and shopping centers and other special gathering places in cities throughout California, the mobile exhibit trailer was remodelled in 1974, filled with natural history exhibits, and sent back out on tour.

In 1969 Mott led the way toward public acquisition and preservation of Allensworth, California, the only town in the state to be founded, financed, and governed by black Americans. An advisory committee made up of historians and others with a special interest in the role of blacks in California history was auhorized by Governor Reagan and appointed by Mott to guide the creation of a masterplan for the acqui-

sition, preservation, and development of Allensworth as a state historic park. By 1972 a preliminary plan had been adopted that called for acquisition of some 240 acres at Allensworth (located some 30 miles north of Bakersfield), plus an extensive program of restoration that would include Colonel Allens-

worth's home and other buildings in the old town. The plan also called for construction of a museum, library, and research center that would tell the story of Colonel Allensworth and other black pioneers and leaders in California history. Despite many disheartening setbacks, supporters of this project re-

Dune buggy, Ocotillo Wells State Vehicular Recreation Area.

Four-wheel-drive racing,
Pismo Dunes State
Vehicular Recreation Area.

fused to give up, and in October 1976, Allensworth State Historic Park was officially dedicated as a unit of the State Park System.

New Funds for the Park System

The Chappie-Z'berg Off-Highway Motor Vehicle Law was approved in 1971 in order to provide a source of funds for the acquisition and development of areas especially designated for off-highway vehicular recreation. The program called for off-highway motor vehicles to be registered—at a cost of $15 every other year—in exchange for the privilege of using California's pub-

lic lands. The Department of Parks and Recreation was to administer this new program, and was charged with developing a statewide plan for the provision of suitable facilities. The Department of Motor Vehicles was to collect registration fees; the Department of Parks and Recreation was to acquire, develop, and operate specially designed vehicular recreation areas, and provide grants to local agencies for the same purposes.

The program got off to a slow start because of the reluctance of many off-road vehicle owners and operators to buy the required permits. Although there were an estimated 1.5 to 2 million off-road vehicles in California, only 102,000 permits were issued during the first two years of the program's operation. Many off-highway vehicle owners were reluctant to pay for something they had taken for granted as free, and some were skeptical that the program would ever amount to anything. Still others including many longtime conservationists, felt that the state, and especially the Department of Parks and Recreation, should not permit or encourage off-highway vehicular recreation in any way. Heated debates took place in public hearings before the State Park and Recreation Commission and elsewhere as to the appropriateness of using certain areas for vehicular recreation. The classification of Red Rock Canyon, for example, resulted in prolonged controversy.

Vehicular recreation interests wanted Red Rock Canyon designated as a

"state vehicular recreation area" that would be entirely open to vehicular use. Others called for state park status and a ban on off-road vehicular use, arguing that scenic and scientific values in the area would be destroyed by the operation of off-road vehicles. The problem was finally resolved to the satisfaction of most parties when Red Rock Canyon was designated a state recreation area in which motor vehicles were welcome to use designated routes of travel everywhere except in several large "natural reserves" that would protect the most important scenic, paleontological, and wildlife values in the region.

As of 1973 five local vehicular recreation projects had been selected for funding, and with income from fees accumulating more rapidly, the state proceeded with plans for the acquisition and development of several state vehicular recreation areas, starting with one in the north and one in the south.

In 1972 and 1973 an unexpected surplus of funds in the state treasury made it possible for the legislature to allocate some $71.5 million for acquisition and development of the State Park System. Known as the Bagley Conservation Fund in honor of the principal author of the legislation, Assemblyman William T. Bagley, this money was earmarked for use in conjunction with some 40 state park acquisition projects including expansion of Point Mugu and Mount Diablo State Parks, further acquisitions along the Sonoma Coast, Kings Beach at Lake Tahoe, Candlestick Point near San Francisco, Simi Valley in Ventura County, Huntington Beach, the Santa Monica Mountains, the Wilder Ranch in Santa Cruz County, and Empire Mine in Nevada County.

Assemblyman Bagley also was the principal author of 1972 legislation that made it possible to appropriate up to $900,000 of gas tax money each year for roads within state parks.
On August 15, 1972 Governor Reagan signed Assembly Bill 392 which had been introduced by Assemblyman Ed Z'berg and approved almost unanimously by the legislature. Known as the "State Beach, Park, Recreational and Historical Facilities Bond Act of 1974," the legislation called for a vote

Old Sacramento State Historic Park. Governor Reagan speaking at ceremony marking the beginning of construction, April 1969. Below: Reconstruction and demolition gets underway in Old Sacramento behind an all-purpose state park boundary sign, 1969.

of the people on June 4, 1974 on a $250 million bond issue. This new bond act was needed, it was argued, because "present outdoor recreational facilities in California are inadequate and will become critically inadequate in the future."

The state would spend a total of $160 million for purchase and development of wildlife preserves ($10 million), for development of historical sites ($15 million), for state park land acquisition ($90 million), and for development of park land already acquired ($45 million). The remaining $90 million would be spent by cities, counties, and other local agencies according to a system of priorities approved by the State Park Commission no later than June 30, 1975. All expenditures under the bond act were to be clearly specified in advance of the vote in June 1974, an approach that, it was hoped, would avoid the kind of legislative cross-fire over park acquisition matters that had troubled Drury's last years as director, and darkened many a debate over 1964 bond fund expenditures.

A short but vigorous campaign on behalf of the 1974 bond act was led by "Californians for Parks, Beaches and Wildlife," whose state chairman was Bill Lane, publisher of *Sunset Magazine* and a well-known outdoorsman. On April 18, 1974 at Lane's expense, a full-page ad appeared in the west coast edition of the *Wall Street Journal* under the heading: "How to realize $250 million on an investment of $350,000." The ad invited California businessmen to help in raising $350,000 for use in the campaign for Proposition One, the 1974 State Park Bond Act. The ad suggested that companies contribute one to five dollars for each of their employees: "By giving on behalf of each employee —and letting them know about it—you affirm that management stands with them and their families on a matter of immediate importance.... The simple truth is that California's parks and beaches are in danger of losing one of their major reasons for being. The opportunity to separate ourselves from the crowd. To renew ourselves. To forget the world of business and concrete and rushing. You can't do that in a park jam-packed with visitors." Passage of Proposition One was especially urgent in light of the "soaring costs of desirable land," and the probability that "what we don't buy today we may not be able to afford tomorrow."

Although no organized opposition had made itself evident, Lane, Mott, and other supporters of the bond act worried that people would vote "no" simply because they did not know enough about Proposition One. For several weeks prior to the election, therefore, Mott toured the state visiting newspaper editors, chambers of commerce, and radio and TV stations in order to make them more aware of the needs of the State Park System. Most of his time was spent in southern California where so many voters are concentrated. When major newspaper and other media people seemed reluctant to endorse Proposition One, Mott spent his time visiting small papers—small dailies and even weeklies—and some of the smaller radio and TV stations. His reception on this level was almost invariably enthusiastic, and widespread support for the park bonds soon became apparent. Before the campaign was over, even the more conservative media spokesmen came out in support of the $250 million bond issue.

In May the governor himself hit the campaign trail on behalf of Proposition One. In three highly publicized appearances, Governor Reagan praised the State Park System for the job it was already doing, and asked the voters to make it possible for the state to preserve more of California's heritage and provide still greater recreational opportunity for everyone.

On June 4, 1974 the people of California once again voted in favor of improving and expanding their State Park System. The final vote—a 60 percent plurality—was 2,525,776 to 1,694,569 in favor of Proposition One.

STATE PARK
ALL PLANTS AND WILDLIFE
PROTECTED

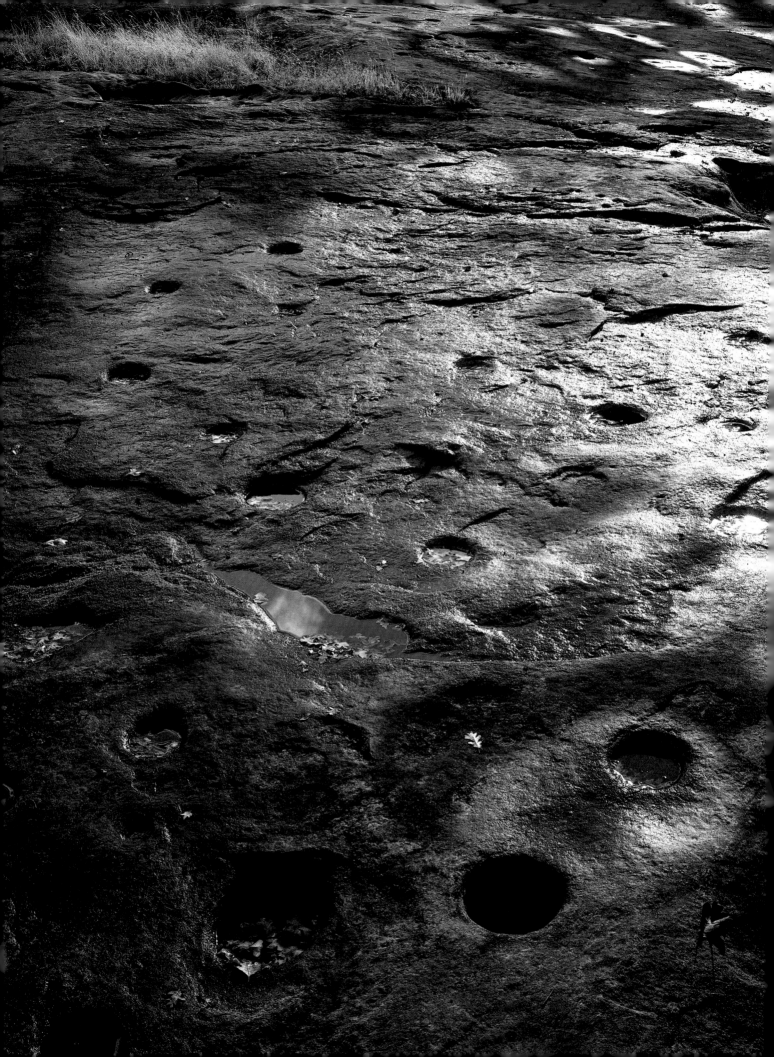

9 The Present and the Future

"As inheritors of a spacious, virgin continent we have had strong roots in the soil and a tradition that should give us special understanding of the mystique of people and land. It is our relationship with the American earth that is being altered by the quiet crisis, our birthright of fresh landscapes and far horizons. Unless we are to betray our heritage consciously, we must make an all-out effort now to acquire the public lands which present and future generations need. Only prompt action will save prime park, forest, and shoreline and other recreation lands before they are preempted for other uses or priced beyond the public purse."

Stewart Udall,
The Quiet Crisis, *1963*

Bedrock mortar,
Indian Grinding Rock
State Historic Park.

Over the years the California State Park System has grown more or less steadily until today it includes some 250 separate units—parks, historic parks, and recreation areas—that, taken together, comprise slightly over one million acres. Total capital investment in this system of parks is nearly one billion dollars, though it should be remembered that the current cash value of the park system would be far higher, and total *real* value is literally beyond calculation.

The extraordinary diversity of California's natural landscape is well represented within the State Park System. There are desert parks, high mountain parks, forest parks, wilderness areas, scenic and natural reserves, sandy beaches, lakes and streams and waterfalls and rivers. More than 200 miles of the magnificent California coastline are now under State Park System management and open to public use. And there are some 500 miles of lake frontage and 87 miles of river frontage. Public service facilities within these areas include museums and visitor centers, hundreds of interpretive exhibits, some 14,000 campsites, 7,584 picnic sites, and approximately 1,500 miles of riding and hiking trails. Historical parks as well as historic sites and buildings within other kinds of state parks and recreation areas preserve a wide range of historical values including Indian village sites and artifacts, Spanish and Mexican period missions, forts, and haciendas. More recent events and people and ways of life are commemorated by state park areas such as the Gold Discovery Site at Coloma, Hearst San Simeon, Jack London's home at Glen Ellen, Bidwell Mansion in Chico, the old State capitol at Benicia, and many others.

It is a truly magnificent park system—the result of foresight and devoted public service on the part of countless people over several generations. By most accounts it is the best state park system in the nation. And yet it is not complete. Nor is it all that it needs to be in order to serve all the people of California.

There are many reasons why the demand for parks and recreational opportunity has continued to outstrip supply. For one thing, human population has doubled over the last 30 years while State Park System acreage has increased by only 60 percent. Meanwhile, modern technology and industrialization have dramatically increased available leisure time, mobility, and spendable income for millions of people. Local park and recreation programs have not been able to keep pace with these changes, and in many urban areas recreational opportunity has actually diminished as open space near the central city has been eliminated by urban sprawl.

As a result of these and other factors, public use of the State Park System over the last 30 years has increased 1,100 percent to some 66 million visitations per year. Demand for park and recreation opportunities has grown so rapidly that, despite all efforts to provide adequate facilities, at least one million would-be park visitors are turned away each year. And the turnaway factor is, after all, only one rather obvious and unsophisticated measure of the real public need for more and better park and recreation opportunity.

An unknown number of people do not even try to use state park areas. Some of them, especially the young, the old, the poor, and the handicapped, find it difficult or impossible to get to the state parks; in an automobile-dominated society they simply lack adequate mobility. Other people, especially members of various racial and ethnic populations, feel that the State Park System simply isn't meant for them. They don't feel entirely welcome, and they look upon the system as largely white and middleclass, irrelevant to their experience and unrelated to their traditional needs and interests. During the last few years such problems as these have been the subject of special effort. But much remains to be done.

Recent Developments

After eight years of avowedly conservative Republican control under Ronald Reagan, the governor's office changed hands January 6, 1975 when Edmund G. Brown, Jr. was inaugurated. Having promised to bring a "new spirit" to state government, Brown's early actions as governor attracted great interest. As part of the transition process, an $11 billion budget was submitted to the legislature, and some 2,200 people

121

Herbert Rhodes

Huey Johnson,
Russell W. Cahill

were appointed to top-level positions in state government. In March this massive appointments process brought Herbert Rhodes to the position of director, Department of Parks and Recreation, replacing Mott. The appointment was a surprise to almost everyone because Rhodes' experience in the field of parks and recreation was quite limited and he was not known by park and recreation professionals in California. A career enlisted man in the U.S. Army until 1955 when a Korean War combat injury cost him his left arm, Rhodes' official involvement in environmental matters included membership on the Central Regional Coastal Commission, and the East Palo Alto Municipal Council. His previous professional experience included seven years as a personnel administrator and training coordinator at Stanford University.

When queried about his relative lack of experience in park and recreation matters, Rhodes responded forthrightly that he would be "the first to admit that I have a lot to learn." On the other hand, he said, he was flexible, open to new ideas, and especially interested in urban parks—in providing more opportunities for disadvantaged young people to escape the crowding and congestion of the city and discover the beauty and refreshing qualities of the natural world. "I want to let them learn about nature so we can hope they will be the saviors of nature, not the destroyers."

"Let's face it," he said in another interview. "I bring something to the job that's never been here before. I've been poor most of my life. I've worked with the poor. I know the contaminated neighborhoods people live in." And state parks, he said, don't help the people who need help most of all because "they're just too far away for the poor people to get to. But maybe you have to come from my side of the fence to see that."

True to his word, Rhodes paid a great deal of attention to the question of urban parks and park programs that would be relevant to the needs of disadvantaged urban populations throughout the state. He hired consultants to carry out a new research project entitled "The California Study on Urban Open Space and Recreation Needs." He and one of his deputies, Alice Wright-Cottingim, set up a new public involvement program—18 public meetings and three public hearings—in order to formulate a comprehensive park and recreation plan for the Santa Monica Mountains near Los Angeles. They also spearheaded State Park System efforts to acquire Candlestick Point near San Francisco, and an important 337-acre parcel of land on San Bruno Mountain in South San Francisco. Development funds were earmarked, insofar as possible, for state parks near urban populations. Rhodes also worked closely with David Roberti and Ed Z'berg on

legislation whereby the department would be able to give increased support to local park and recreation agencies in urban areas. As approved by the legislature in May 1976, the Roberti-Z'berg Urban Open Space and Recreation Program provided $25 million a year for three years for grants to cities, counties, and local park and recreation districts, with the state contributing 75 percent of the cost of each project.

During Rhodes' tenure as director of the Department of Parks and Recreation, progress was also made in the field of off-highway vehicular recreation. One hundred miles of trail were developed at Hollister Hills State Vehicular Recreation Area in central California, and on June 12, 1976 the area was formally dedicated to public use. Hungry Valley near Gorman (about 50 miles north of downtown Los Angeles), was selected as the site for a major southern California off-highway vehicular recreation area and, despite continuing controversy, plans for acquisition and development of the site were begun. An increasing number of grants were awarded to local agencies for off-highway vehicular recreation purposes, and in the spring of 1977 the first such recreation area to be completed using funds from the Chappie-Z'berg legislation of 1971—the River Front O.H.V. facility in Marysville—was finally opened to the public.

Affirmative action was also an im-

Jacqueline Stewart, a spokesperson for the Miwok people associated with Chaw'se, Indian Grinding Rock State Historic Park. Right: Visitor Center at Chaw'se, August 1977.

Former Director Rhodes, Chief Deputy Director Alice Wright-Cottingim, Director Cahill, Former Director Mott at the Governor's Mansion Centennial Celebration, December 1977.

portant focus of the Rhodes administration. Hiring goals were set with an eye to bringing departmental employment patterns more into line with statewide work force patterns. Since most rangers and park maintenance workers tend to be chosen from among those first hired as seasonal employees, a set of goals was established for the hiring of seasonals: starting in the spring of 1977, 23 percent of all temporary positions were to be filled by ethnic minorities; 35 percent were to be women.

As called for by the Equal Employment Act of 1972 and Title VII of the Civil Rights Act of 1964, and in response to state guidelines covering affirmative action programs, a department-wide affirmative action plan was approved by the State Personnel Board and put into effect March 15, 1977. In keeping with this plan, a new category of ranger—the "park technician"—was created in order to allow more women and ethnic minorities to enter the state park ranger ranks.

At the end of June 1977, Governor Brown made a number of changes in his administration, one of which brought Huey Johnson to the position of Resources Agency Secretary. Soon afterward, Johnson decided to bring in a park system management team of his own choosing. As a result, Russell W. Cahill was appointed director of the Department of Parks and Recreation on September 2, 1977. Resources Secretary Johnson was quick to applaud Herb Rhodes for his accomplishments, and to insist that under Cahill, the Department of Parks and Recreation would continue to pursue all of the programs Rhodes had launched, and would maintain its affirmative action goals, its relatively new urban emphasis, and its more traditional objectives. Preserving some remnant of the great American wilderness heritage through the creation of public parks was, Johnson said, uniquely important and American. "There is nothing else like it. Europe, for instance, can't even come up with wild natural parks. The opportunities there were wiped out long, long ago." The wilderness aspect of the park program in California and in America generally was so important, he said, that "in the future, perhaps 600 years from now, an even more crowded and heavily urbanized population may well

look back on this as the era when parks and the concept of parks was created." This would be parallel, he pointed out, to the historical judgment we make today when we look back 600 years to Michelangelo and the other great artists of his time whose work has come to symbolize the era we now refer to as the Renaissance.

According to Johnson, the park movement also had to meet current social and urban realities face on; there could be "no retreat." And he was confident that the department under Russ Cahill would continue to strive—as it had under Herb Rhodes—toward fulfillment of both its immediate social responsibilities and its obligation to future generations.

At 39 years of age, Cahill was the youngest person ever appointed director of the Department of Parks and Recreation. He nevertheless brought some 17 years of governmental experience to his new assignment. Born and raised in California and the holder of a degree in biology, Cahill had begun his career in parks in 1966 as a ranger in Yosemite National Park. In January 1971, after a number of other assignments with the National Park Service, he was named superintendent of Haleakala National Park in Hawaii. From 1975 to 1977 he served as director of parks for the state of Alaska. His strong personal affinity for wilderness conditions was evident in his work for the National Park Service. He also took a year off

Dedication of Colonel Allensworth State Historic Park, October 1976. Below, left: Director Rhodes, State Park Ranger Al Griffin, Advisory Committee Chairman Dr. Kenneth Goode. Right: Josephine B. Smith, grandaughter of Colonel Allensworth.

from park work to build a cabin and live with his family—simply, primitively—on a remote homestead near Glacier Bay in Alaska. Once on the job in California, however, he devoted special attention to the park and recreation needs of urban disadvantaged people, especially racial and ethnic minorities.

In May 1978, at Big Basin Redwoods State Park, speaking to a gathering of park professionals and activists on the occasion of the State Park System's 50th Anniversary celebration, he described his point of view this way: "I look around today and I see a people out of touch: out of touch with nature, out of touch with their history, out of touch with each other." Even in the parks, he said, in the convenience-filled campgrounds of the modern state or national park, the silence and serenity of the natural environment, the laughter of children, and the hum of adult conversation were likely to be overwhelmed by the electronic chatter of portable radios and TV sets. The "mission" of the park movement should be, he said, "to put people back in touch with the real world and with each other. The parks must once again become places for communication with nature,

with other people, and with ourselves. With the encouragement of that communication should come an enlightened people who can make more rational choices about our Earth."

He was concerned, moreover, that "national and state parks, those great treasure houses of all the *peoples* of this country, are not used by all of the *peoples* of this country." Black people, Mexican-American people, Asian people and members of other racial or ethnic minorities would use the parks and benefit from them only if they felt welcome. The answer, he said, was simple: "You and I must make them more comfortable in the parks through our publications, our interpretive programs, and through employment of minority employees in a fair approximation of California's population percentages. That is our major challenge."

In keeping with this point of view, Cahill promoted Alice Wright-Cottingim to be his chief deputy director. The first black woman to hold such a high level position in the Department of Parks and Recreation, Wright-Cottingim had been greatly taken with the park movement, and was delighted by her opportunity to serve the needs of the people through parks while serving as a consultant and later as a deputy director under Herb Rhodes. Cahill also saw to it — as Rhodes had done before him—that the makeup of the State Park and Recreation Commission was broadened to include a representative range of ethnic backgrounds. Affirmative action programs within the department were accelerated, and the department's role in urban affairs was expanded.

Old Sacramento State Historic Park. Facing page: *Northwestern Pacific locomotive 112 was built in 1908 by the American Locomotive Works, Schenectedy, New York and used to haul passenger trains in the north coast redwood region, 1908 to 1953.*

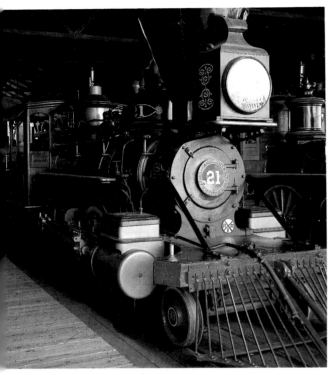

Left: *Virginia & Truckee Railroad locomotive 21, the "J. W. Bowker." Built in 1875 for use on the Comstock Lode, Nevada, and later used to haul lumber at Lake Tahoe, 1896 to 1917. Featured in Cecil B. DeMille's 1939 film "Union Pacific."* Above: *Exterior of the Central Pacific Passenger Station, western terminus (1896) of the nation's first transcontinental railroad. Re-created as a central feature of Old Sacramento State Historic Park.* Below: *North end of the Passenger Station.*

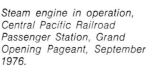

Senator Albert Rodda, Director Rhodes, State Parks Foundation President Mott, and Southern Pacific Vice-President Larry Hoyt.

Steam engine in operation, Central Pacific Railroad Passenger Station, Grand Opening Pageant, September 1976.

An "Urban Interpretive Program" unit was created within the department, for example. This program was designed to link environmental education with opportunities to work in the field of parks and recreation, so that disadvantaged young people from selected "urban impacted areas" would be able to learn about environmental matters while simultaneously gaining practical work experience serving as student interns, volunteers, or temporary employees of state and local park and recreation agencies. The program was intended not only to expose disadvantaged inner city young people to a wide range of parks and park-related employment possibilities, but also to set up new lines of communication as young people involved in the program took the park story back to their families and friends in the ghetto and the inner city. This kind of communication could play an important role in breaking down what Cahill described as "the subtle barriers that separate millions of our state's citizens from their natural and historical heritage."

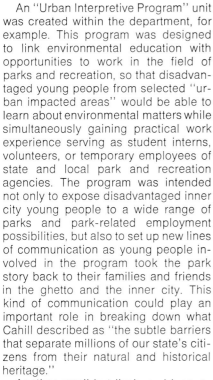

Another small but lively and innovative program, the "Urban Action Team," was also set up within the Department of Parks and Recreation by Cahill. It was designed to facilitate private sector involvement in park and recreation projects on the local level, and to locate nontraditional funding sources for recreation programs hard hit by cutbacks in local property tax revenues after the passage of Proposition 13, the "Jarvis-Gann Initiative," in June 1978.

The political climate surrounding the Jarvis-Gann "tax revolt" of 1978 put a damper on government programs of all kinds, but did not diminish public enthusiasm and support for the State Park System. On the contrary, impatience with delays in state park acquisition and development programs continued to mount. And controversy over park matters was likely to focus not on whether there should be more parks, but on which park projects should come first given the limited funds available.

Public support for expansion and improvement of the park system had been expressed in the park bond acts of 1964, 1968, and 1974. Continuing support was evident in the passage of the $280 million Coastal Bond Act of 1976 which was approved at the polls

after only the most cursory of campaigns on its behalf. This bond issue was a direct response to the mandate for coastal preservation as called for by the Coastal Zone Conservation Commission, but funds were also provided for inland park projects including preservation and restoration of historical sites, and the development of further recreational facilities at State Water Project reservoirs. The need to provide still more funding for park acquisition and development, possibly by means of another bond act, was discussed by the legislature in 1979; but with inflation undermining the value of bond issues almost as fast as the people could approve them at the polls, and with the price of desirable land increasing at an especially rapid rate, the need for a simpler, faster, more efficient acquisition procedure was obvious.

Recognizing the seriousness of this problem, Cahill and the department made an all-out effort to overcome the many stumbling blocks in the acquisition process. State-mandated procedures for park land acquisition had become even more complex and time-consuming than they were during the mid-1950s when public (and legislative) impatience with the program had first become widespread. The answer, as Cahill explained to the governor and the legislature, was to simplify the process, reduce the role of the Department of Finance, the Public Works Board, and others, and give the Department of Parks and Recreation a greater degree of direct control over park acquisition matters.

While park system acquisition questions were being debated, a number of milestones in the history of the system were celebrated. On March 16, 1979, a new visitor center was dedicated in Anza-Borrego Desert State Park. The fulfillment of a long-held dream, this 7,000-square-foot orientation and interpretive center is not only a handsome and practical addition to the park; it is a monument to the vision, persistence, and generosity of the Anza-Borrego Desert Natural History Association and many other private individuals and corporations including the California State Parks Foundation. Fully half of the million dollars needed for construction was provided from private sources. Moreover, staffing for the new visitor

center was to be handled largely by a corps of 75 unpaid volunteers, all of whom take a nine-week training course in order to become qualified docents.

The building itself is unique. Half buried in the desert floor and featuring native materials and other carefully considered adaptations to the desert environment, the building was designed by San Diego architect Robert Donald Ferris working closely with Harry Daniel, president of the Natural History Association, and others both in and outside the Department of Parks and Recreation. Exhibits in the building are designed to help the park visitor figure out how to explore the fascinating, spacious, and age-old ways of an environment that most urban dwellers, especially those from California's coastal cities, are apt to consider ominous and forbidding.

Another milestone in State Park System interpretive efforts was passed on April 21, 1979 when festive groundbreaking ceremonies celebrated the beginning of construction of the new California State Railroad Museum. Located beside the Sacramento River on the site of the western terminus of the nation's first transcontinental railroad, the new $14 million, 94,000-square-foot museum is scheduled for completion in the early 1980s. It will be—according to expert opinion—both the largest and the finest railroad history museum in the United States. This ambitious project represents years of planning plus generous contributions of rolling stock and other artifacts from private sources. As Cahill put it, "The museum is the largest single development ever undertaken by the State Park System. It will make Old Sacramento a mecca for railroad history students and enthusiasts throughout the world." Already the reconstruction and restoration of historic buildings in Old Sacramento State Historic Park, plus a delightful blend of commercial development and historical interpretation, have brought new life to what was until recently a sadly decayed portion of downtown Sacramento.

Another momentous groundbreaking ceremony occurred on the first of May 1979, when construction got underway on California's first "urban state park" at Candlestick Point in San Francisco. Mayor Dianne Feinstein referred to the

Architect and consultant Barry Howard, Supervisor of Interpretive Services Norm Wilson (pointing), and Alice Wright-Cottingim, April 1977. On the table: a scale model of the proposed Museum of Railroad History, the third and final phase of development of Old Sacramento State Historic Park.

project as "a major recreational resource," that would make the nearby, poverty stricken, Bayview-Hunters Point residential area more livable and more "viable economically." While looking forward to large-scale future development, plans for the area also called for "immediate public use" facilities to be developed by California Conservation Corps workers. Meanwhile, plans for the acquisition and development of other "urban state parks," including Willowbrook State Recreation Area in Los Angeles, were also proceeding.

For Future Generations

Throughout untold millions of years Man has evolved on this planet as a uniquely upright, uniquely clever observer of the natural world. As a result, Man the hunter, the collector, the wanderer, the nest builder, the inventor, artist, and philosopher, has managed to survive fire and flood, tempest and drought, and even the grinding hardship of an ice age that recently brought extinction to many of Earth's creatures.

Still more recently, however, in what amounts to only the barest flicker of evolutionary and geologic time, Man has invented and moved into an environment that is largely of his own making — the modern, industrialized city. And suddenly we are face to face with the possibility that Man may be domesticating himself—losing touch with the great natural realities that have shaped human life throughout the ages.

It might be argued that the broad tendency toward domestication, toward complete preoccupation with social and manufactured realities, has been accompanied by an ever greater technical understanding and technological control of the world around us. And certainly the dazzling technological accomplishments of our time are ample support for that argument. But we must never disregard Man's other needs whatever they may be—spiritual, emotional, philosophical, perhaps even physiological — for continuing contact with nature.

In his Yosemite report of 1865, Frederick Law Olmsted maintained it was "a scientific fact that the occasional contemplation of natural scenes" was "favorable to the health and vigor of men and especially the health and vigor of

their intellect beyond any other conditions which can be offered them...." Moreover, he said, those who could afford to do so had always enjoyed the restorative value of such contemplation. For example, he said, "the great men of the Babylonians, the Persians and the Hebrews, had their rural retreats, as large and as luxurious as those of the aristocracy of Europe at present."

But, as Olmsted pointed out, in a democracy it is neither practical nor appropriate to limit the benefits of direct contact with nature to "great men." Government in America had an obligation to ensure that "enjoyment of the choicest natural scenes in the country and the means of recreation connected with them" should never become a monopoly "of a very few, very rich people" nor of any other privileged class.

The governing classes of the old world, according to Olmsted, had considered it necessary to keep the mass of people busy at almost constant labor, while limiting their recreation to such artificial pleasures as "theatres, parades, and promenades where they will be amused by the equipages of the rich and the animation of crowds." On the other hand, Olmsted believed that

Dedication of the Visitor Center, Anza-Borrego Desert State Park, March 1979.

Director Cahill addressing the assembled guests, State Park System 50th Anniversary Celebration in Big Basin, May 1978.

in the new world *everyone* had a right to enjoy the natural scene, and through contemplation, especially contemplation of unmodified natural conditions, to arrive at some independent conclusions about the nature of things. Only on the basis of independent appraisals of the world could individuals in a democracy cast their deciding votes wisely and effectively.

Following this same line of thought, Dr. John C. Merriam later insisted that educational need could never be met "merely in accumulation of facts." The most important aspect of the learning process, he said, was "essentially inspirational.... Human interest in natural phenomena, whether from the point of view of the lover of nature, the investigator, the teacher, or the preacher is of real significance only when the individual is brought face to face with reality, and makes his judgments on the basis of his own personal observations." Merriam believed this kind of learning opportunity could be preserved best of all in state and national parks, that "the purely educational value" of parks was, at least in some ways, "far beyond that of any regularly established formal educational institution.... There are not in America other places where comparable possibilities for effective adult education concerning nature can be found, with the grandest products of creation themselves as teachers."

This same point of view led Colonel Richard Lieber, the moving spirit behind the creation of the Indiana State Park System, to insist that "our parks and preserves are not merely picnicking places. They are rich storehouses of memories and reveries. They are bearers of wonderful tales to him who will listen, a solace to the aged and an inspiration to the young." The same theme was struck many years later by Russ Cahill—at the 50th Anniversary Celebration of the California State Park System in 1978—when he said that parks should be looked upon "not as

curiosity shops or technological data centers, but as touchstones of human and natural history."

It remains to be seen, of course, just how far this point of view can be carried. How far can we go toward providing adequate breathing space and recreational opportunity for *everyone* in this state and nation—including the millions of disadvantaged people who now reside in our great urban centers? How good a job can we do in preserving representative examples of the magnificent natural landscape that has made California world famous? Can we also preserve sufficiently eloquent reminders of California's diverse cultural heritage? (One glaring deficiency in this regard has been California's failure, despite Olmsted's recommendations in 1928, to preserve representative villages and other reminders of the traditions that shaped human experience in this part of the world for thousands of years prior to the arrival of explorers and settlers from Europe.)

The adequacy of our response to these questions is important here in our own time, but will be even more important in the future as population continues to increase, and as technology continues to intervene between human beings and the natural environment. As Dr. Merriam said in 1931 in his dedication address at Founders Grove in Humboldt Redwoods State Park: "The state of civilization of a people may be measured by its care and forethought for the welfare of generations to come."

Looking to the future by the light of past events, one simple and unchanging fact about the California State Park System stands out above all the rest: the program would not have been possible—or at best would have been far less meaningful—without the generous support of private individuals and organizations such as the Save-the-Redwoods League, the Sierra Club, the State Parks Foundation, the Sempervirens Club and its successor the Sempervirens Fund, the Nature Con-

servancy, Conservation Associates, numerous cooperating advisory committees and associations, and countless other groups and individuals. The record shows that this kind of support has continued through thick and thin, regardless of partisan political trends, and has involved so many significant gifts to the State Park System and to the people of California that it is not even possible to list them all in a publication of this kind.

Gifts to the State Park System by the Save-the-Redwoods League alone amount to approximately $31 million, and 136,000 acres of redwood forestland. And there is no sign that support from private sources is abating. In fact, the number of citizens participating in State Park System affairs is increasing and includes people from a broadening range of social, ethnic, economic, and professional backgrounds. It would seem that idealism, as expressed through the park movement, is still alive and well — perhaps even growing stronger—despite the political and economic uncertainties of our time.

The real question, then, about the future of the State Park System is whether people, and the kind of practical idealism that created the park system in the first place, can form new alliances and create new governmental mechanisms that will be adequate to the needs of our democratic society. Success for the park movement, not only in California but across the nation and around the world, will depend on how clearly we perceive the important role parks can play, not only in terms of human pleasure and contentment, but in terms of human survival on an ever-changing planet. If the park movement itself and decision makers in general can be persuaded that the vision of Olmsted and other leaders of the park movement is essentially correct, then the story of parks will only have begun, and park system accomplishments in the future will dwarf those of the past and present.